ARS BREVE VITA LONGA

MOVIES THAT CAME OFF THE SCREEN

DONALD DEWEY

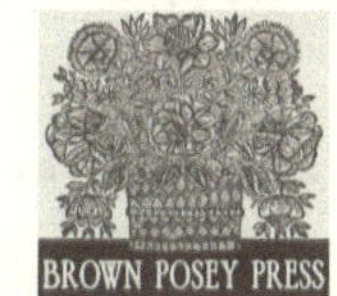

an imprint of Sunbury Press, Inc.
Mechanicsburg, PA USA

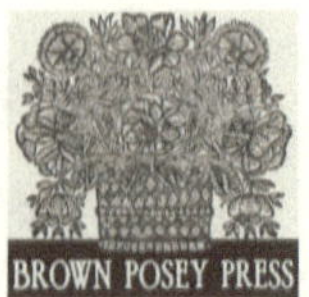

an imprint of Sunbury Press, Inc.
Mechanicsburg, PA USA

FIRST BROWN POSEY PRESS EDITION: November 2021

Set in Adobe Garamond Pro | Interior design by Crystal Devine | Cover design by Lawrence Knorr | Edited by Lawrence Knorr.

Publisher's Cataloging-in-Publication Data
Names: Dewey, Donald, author.
Title: Ars breve vita longa : movies that came off the screen / Donald Dewey.
Description: First trade paperback edition. | Mechanicsburg, PA : Brown Posey Press, 2021.
Summary: *Ars Breve Vita Longa* follows the author's decades-long odyssey through orchestras in the United States and Europe to describe the indelible characters he encountered on and off the screen and that, not just by coincidence, had a strong influence in developing his own character.
Identifiers: ISBN : 978-1-62006-888-5 (softcover).
Subjects: BIOGRAPHY & AUTOBIOGRAPHY / Music | MUSIC / History & Criticism | ART / Film & Video.

Product of the United States of America
0 1 1 2 3 5 8 13 21 34 55

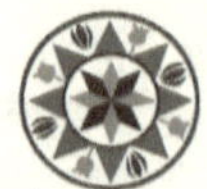

Continue the Enlightenment!

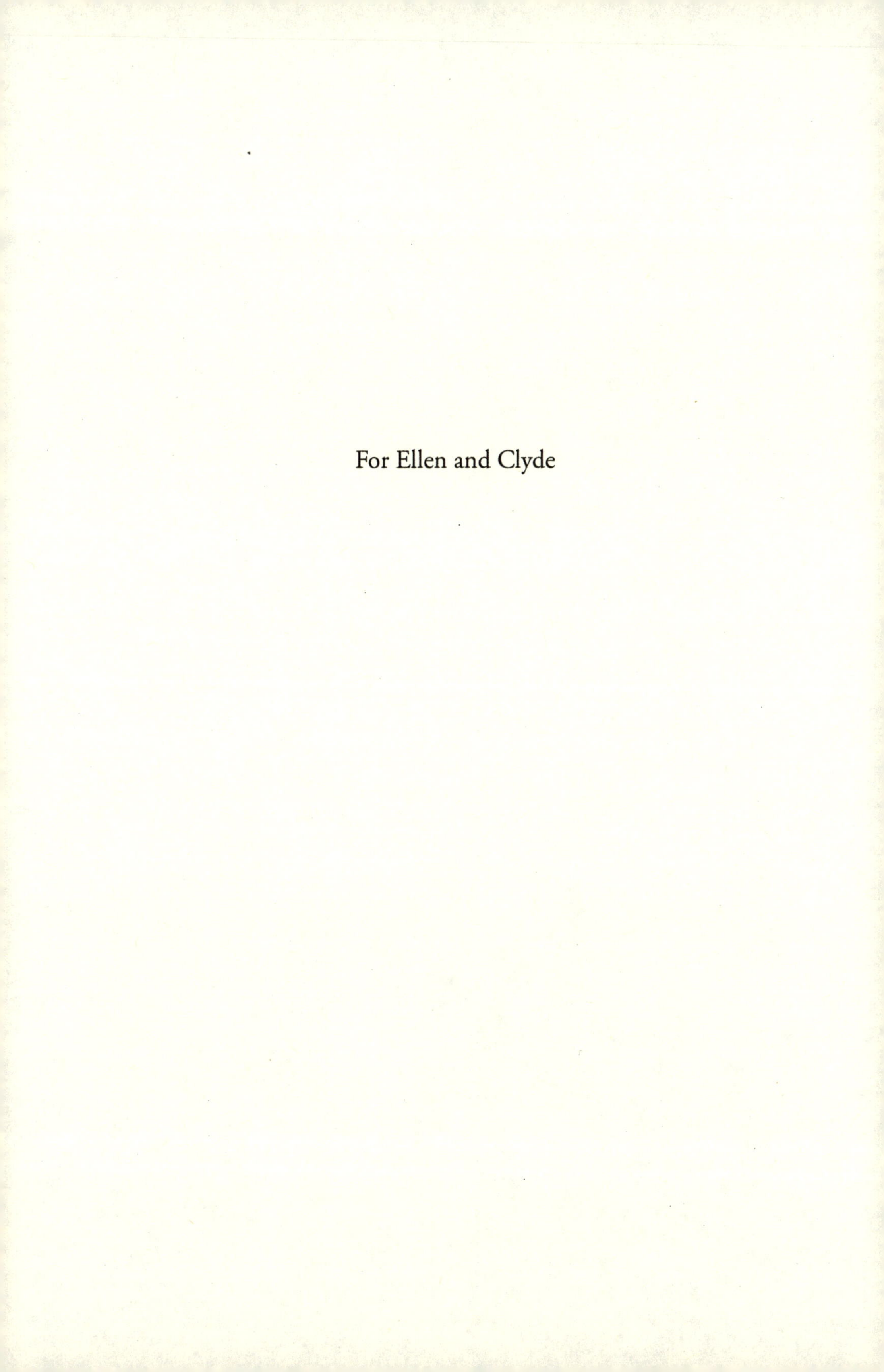

For Ellen and Clyde

CONTENTS

INTRODUCTION

Long before there were multiplexes, before felons developed tactics to pay once for seeing more than one movie, it was still possible to turn a single ticket into a compound investment. And it didn't take a lot of sneaking around lobbies and keeping an eye on stub collectors, either. No ingenuity whatsoever was required.

Of course, there was the movie on the screen in Cinemascope, Vistavision, and any number of variations on technicolor, sepia, and rust. That picture offered an array of action, of dialogue, of musical scoring, of more action, more dialogue, and more musical scoring. The actors were gigantic, the smallest background hill could have been the Alps, and crystalline streams thundered like Niagara Falls. Size, size, and more size. But all the while this picture was playing out before widened eyes, a second one was running for the same single admission—the one being unspooled in our heads. Dot, dot, and more dots.

Boredom was not the only catalyst for the second feature. Yes, it might happen that the learned on-screen discussions of Plato's principles or analyses of Lenin's strategies at Finland Station could promote mental drift. Sometimes it took a striptease to refocus on what was going on at the front of the theater. But even a striptease or an equivalent stampede of thousands of steers goring and stomping on townspeople too slow to get out of their way didn't always restore focus to where the projectionist wanted it to be. Amazing as it was, a second feature between the ears could occasionally overwhelm the first one between the sprockets, and not only because the national budgets splattered over the bigger screen had been spent unwisely.

Association—that was the key. An actor, a look, a situation—what set it off could have been anything, maybe even the unpopped kernel of pop corn antagonizing a cavity. All we had to bring to it was vulnerability, just as any actor had to bring to a scene to make it convincing. And we were more than actors. We were also our own script writers and directors, at times even the spectators when a memory of particular weight awoke a frisson of excitement or depression. A lot of time could elapse from one scene to another, often more than that elapsing on the big screen where a fist fight in a Texas saloon was followed immediately by the roustabouts snarling at one another from separate cells in Romania. Whatever those university film classes had to say, *montage* was not exclusive to *auteurs*. Any brain at all could edit and recompose reality.

Genre was not a problem. Westerns could spark horror shriekers, thrillers, slapstick comedies. It went without saying that we were always the protagonists, for good, bad, and embarrassing. Many of our private features carried such titles as *Oh, God!*, *Did I Really Do That?*, and *I Wonder What Happened to Her.* As for co-stars, they had invariably been swallowed up by time, space, and, in the most melancholy cases, death. Only self-discipline held us back from following the plot into non-movie realms where we lost sight of what had been shot and what we just wished had been. We weren't *that* cavalier about the dollars handed over back at the box office. A double-bill was a double-bill.

We knew we would never win awards for what we had produced, but our features remained far more personal than what the screen upfront, even at its best, was trying to bathe us in. *Vita est longa, ars brevis.*

SLEEP, MY LOVE

Claudette Colbert was always wearing a bow over her blouse even when she wasn't—the sort of chintzy bow hanging off a box of Russell Stover chocolates. There was also that sheen to her apple cheeks, a motif of Sunday restaurant brunches when the main course was Bloody Marys for getting over Saturday night. The bow said Colbert thought of herself as demure, the sheen that she wasn't sure she could keep up that appraisal heading into a maiden aunt age. Was the waiter snickering when he went past her to serve other tables? She wasn't sure.

She had more concrete problems in *Sleep My Love*. She woke up in a New York-to-Boston train with no idea how she had ended up there. A ditzy fellow passenger, maybe not so ditzy, found a gun in her purse, and Colbert didn't know anything about that, either. The compartment was all woo-woo and not from the sound of the locomotive. In the meantime, at Colbert's Sutton Place mansion, husband Don Ameche was doing a bad job of masking an aching arm as he informed a cop that his wife suffered from blackouts and was given to running off without telling him. And yes, she had hurt him this time before going. No, he had no explanation for it, but he worried about her mutterings about suicide. The cop said he could understand why.

I had once had a fence spike go through my arm while trying to climb into a shuttered schoolyard for a softball game. The flap of skin as I had hoisted myself up high enough to pull my arm free had been an essential part of my soundtrack ever since. *Flap, flurp, flurp*. But I noticed a difference between that and Ameche's reaction to his hurt. Willy-nilly, I had accepted my puncture as what I had deserved trying to breech security against thugs using schoolyards after hours. Ameche, though, didn't look in the least remorseful even as he was implicating Colbert in a felony. He looked furtive, evasive, the kind of guy who lied even as he told the truth. There was no doubt that he was responsible for some of the woo-woo back in the train.

It didn't take long to confirm this. Through some kind of fast shuffle of the penal code and plausible drama, Colbert flew back to New York, to her dubiously concerned husband. He wasted no time telling her that she needed a shrink for dealing with her mysterious blackouts. And as luck would have it, he just happened to know one. Sort of.

Meanwhile just take this pill, and you'll get some sleep. Don't pay attention to all his carnival sideshow motions for hypnotizing her. He had gotten them from the same place he had picked up the silk bathrobes and dressing gowns he was addicted to.

Colbert was in no condition to resist. Clearly, she hadn't been since making her mansion and bank accounts part of her marriage to Ameche. You could build up to a headache neuron by neuron, waiting for her to recognize the evil in front of her. Hadn't she seen *Gaslight*? And what about that arch sophisticate who seemed to shop only in the negligee and lacy bra department before egging Ameche on to grander woo-woo? You were pretty sure he had noticed her long legs. And if he wasn't deaf, he had certainly heard her saying things like, "We've got a lot, but we haven't got everything. I want what she's got—all of it." Ameche seemed to think this modest goal was a reasonable price for her long legs. As for Colbert, she might have been rich and in love, but she wasn't bright, rich, and in love. There was a reason for warning labels on bottles, and she was it.

Then things got *very* serious. Colbert went to the shrink Ameche had recommended. As embodied by the squirrely George Coulouris, he was far too obviously someone with a shingle for abetting suicide rather than heading it off. One tipoff was that his glasses were thick enough to monitor what was happening on nearby planets. The good news for the psychiatric profession was that he wasn't one of theirs but a photographer brought into Ameche's scheme for driving Colbert to suicide and himself to the lease of the Sutton Place mansion. The bad news for Colbert was that Coulouris had a daffy wife seen previously discovering a gun in a train compartment and had a model who bought a lot of negligees and lacy bras. The walls were beginning to close in on the only person who failed to notice they were. She remembered only what she had forgotten. I was beginning to envy her. There was something a little bit too familiar about the painful brooding up on the screen.

My toothache was an uncomfortable memory. I recalled only too well how it had started one night after supper as a trickle that still could have been talked out of turning into the Mississippi. As long as I kept my tongue away from it (which, of course, I didn't), I told myself it would go away on its own, no dentists and their metal sticks required. A day of fire later, I was told my dentist was on vacation, so I had to make an appointment with the one filling in for him. The first trouble was that the substitute wasn't operating out of my regular dentist's office but from his own, and that was downtown in a gloomy neighborhood where only the garbage cans looked at home. I thought about Moloch, Baal, and the other gods who would have made keeping my appointment unnecessary. But they all turned out to be on vacation, too.

Colbert tried to look as pleased as I would have been in entering Dr. Coulouris's office. Her first discovery was that he was as much of a fan of pills and hypnosis as her husband. That made her suspicious, but not being bright, she didn't know of what. What disconcerted her more was that outside the office window was an elevated subway that shuttled back and forth from Hell with sparks beneath the wheels to prove it. This made for hallucinatory lights coming in the window and reflecting off the doctor's thick glasses. Since the nearby planets had moved into the doctor's office, Colbert couldn't depend on sympathy even from the furthest reaches of the galaxy. She had every reason to feel cosmically alone.

At least Colbert was dry, which was more than I could say for myself and the half-dozen others crammed into the dentist's waiting room one rainy evening. The stench of mercurochrome hanging over the umbrella dankness was bad enough. Worse were two bleary table lamps that provided glazing light to suggest that phenomenon but not quite demonstrating it and a legion of hooded Ku Klux Klan shadows they threw up on the walls. Worst of all were the thunderclaps outside the waiting room's single window and the protests of a nine-year-old girl with every boom and her mother's stern warning that there was no way she was going to get out of seeing the dentist. I really didn't need the mother smiling at me conspiratorially every time she issued that edict. I didn't belong to her lying scheme or anybody else's. I would not have known what to do with a Sutton Place mansion even if I had one.

Colbert tried to assure herself she felt fine after her visit with Dr. Coulouris. She even smiled thankfully to her husband when she returned to her mansion. What was harder to figure out came some hours later when she found herself on her balcony bent on diving down to Sutton Place cabs. She had the dazed look of someone who had been taking a psychiatrist's advice from a photographer. Luckily, she had help working out her trance at the last second from Robert Cummings, whom she had met on the plane taking her back to New York from Boston and who had been intrigued by her amnesia and blouse bow. When the part was for a table leaf of a character (useful but necessary only every so often), Cummings's overaged preppie presence was ideal, especially when there was a whimpering wife in danger from a homicidal husband (see also *Dial M for Murder*). Not only did he get out to the balcony in time to prevent Colbert's dive, but she began to see that all men didn't wear dressing gowns and rush to hypnotize her. She began to look oddly at Ameche, and he didn't like the look. If there was one thing geared to ruining his day, it was awareness.

My dentist was not reassuring. He was too knobby—all knees and elbows, even his hands more knuckles than fingers. And then there were his eyes. He might have been overworked from adding the regular patients of my dentist to his own; certainly, his waiting room reeked of a cattle pen. Or he might have just been weary examining gums all his life. Either way, bloodshot did not cover his corneal problem, his eyes instead calling to mind the peppermint button candies in reception desk bowls. He was definitely grateful to be able to sit at a corner desk and shut his eyes for a respite while a nurse took care of the X-raying of the tooth that had brought us together. It wasn't the moment for me to think of Renfield visiting Count Dracula, but I did anyway.

Cummings's untimely appearance on the balcony caused a lot of irritation among Ameche and his friends. The model with the long legs became particularly snappish, blaming Coulouris for having hypnotized Colbert ineffectively and addressing him as "Four Eyes." Coulouris didn't take to this generously and wondered—humorlessly, it has to be said—what she had been contributing to their scheme. The photographer's wife thought it was all a little amusing, as though she had known from the start that bad things happened to bad people. Ameche kept thoughts between himself and his dressing gown. He was clearly thinking of an improvisation that involved his accomplices more than they would be enthusiastic about.

The X-rays were bad, Dracula's extraction decision worse. The nurse's sarcastic SHISH might have come from an assistant who had never heard anything else out of his mouth. Or was that a choral hiss of lust from Dracula's virgins down in the catacombs? Never mind, the priority for the moment was to focus on the needle Dracula held theatrically over my face just in case I was thinking of ignoring it. And to make doubly sure I didn't jump up from the chair, one of his knobby knees pressed down on my thigh, a hold he had apparently learned watching wrestling on TV. I took the high road, deciding it was just a tactic for diverting attention from the needle. It didn't really work.

Cummings didn't stop at saving Colbert on the balcony. He made little pretense of being interested in Ameche's social chatter, all but calling him a liar at one point. More disastrously for those scheming to take over the mansion, he tracked down the genuine psychiatrist whose name Coulouris had been using. Even Colbert began to catch on at this point. But Ameche hadn't fallen to sleep, either. If he couldn't have Colbert crashing down on a taxi, what about the cops arresting her for killing a photographer, passing himself off as a shrink, and using hypnosis to push her to suicide? With her behind bars, he would have still had the mansion. Long legs had no objection. Hadn't she made it clear she was bored posing for Four Eyes? Who would miss a photographer with suspect vision?

The Novocaine took too long and not long enough to kick in. Through the wait Dracula and the nurse whispered, whisper-argued, then whispered some more. I was no fan of his peppermint buttons, but I wouldn't have minded if he had turned them back toward me every so often, so I didn't get the feeling they were afraid of showing the tortures they had in mind on their faces. When the numbness did finally arrive, there was still too much uncoated feeling on the roof of my mouth. Did that mean Dracula hadn't stuck his needle in the right spot, that his striped eyeballs had settled for being close? Who wanted to be thinking that while taking the high road?

Ameche committed the classic mistake of the would-be perfect murderer—overthinking. Colbert didn't want to gun down Coulouris, Coulouris didn't want to be gunned down by Colbert, but Ameche saw those objections dismissed by hypnosis. Wrong. Coulouris saw what was afoot and turned a revolver of his own on Ameche. Things were getting messy.

Everywhere. The pliers in front of my face for yanking my tooth were not supposed to look so much like pliers, those clamps for pulling out nails on horseshoes, but they did. And the way the Count's hand shook in holding them said I hadn't been off about how approximate he had been about the needle. Did the nurse stand directly behind my chair to give him parameters for a better aim? He disabused me of that idea by nodding to her on what looked like their prearranged signal. At once, her big arms came around the chair to wrap me into a statue. Not only did the Count like wrestling, but he was also partial to the tag team kind! I wanted a train to rumble through the window to smother any screaming, but I had to settle for cracks inside my mouth that sounded like the cars cracking through track buffers. Woo-woo!

Cummings arrived too late to stop the aggrieved Coulouris from shooting Ameche. But he still had time to chase after the photographer across a rooftop or two until finally sending him to his death through a skylight. The glass fragments laying around might have been from the skylight or Coulouris's thick glasses or maybe even from distant planets. Shards had never looked *shardier*, but I had lost much more blood than

Coulouris. It was all over my paper bib, the back of Dracula's knobby hand, and the guilty pliers. The liquid oozing from my mouth didn't feel like Seven-Up, either.

"He broke my fucking finger!"

Dracula's reaction was to look apprehensively toward the waiting room in case somebody still waiting heard something disagreeable. He was absolutely quaint in the way he shook his head to the nurse and put a finger to his lips for her to shut up. The nurse didn't see it in any case. She was holding out her left index finger from behind me like some part of her body she wanted somebody to take off her and dispose of.

"You fucking maniac! You broke it!"

"I'm sure it's not broken," the Count ventured.

"You are, heh? Give me your finger, and we'll see."

The Count ignored the offer to return interest to me with more of the wads of cotton that seemed to be growing from the dental instrument tray.

"I'm going to sue you, you bastard."

"Jill, please!"

I didn't know enough about the law to know if Jill could sue me for cracking her index finger. I didn't even know if Dracula was legally responsible for the cleaning bill, thanks to the blood trickling off my bib onto my shirt. What I did know was that the new hole in my cheek was aching just fine without the smeared tooth now sitting proud and nasty on the instrument tray.

"Get him those pills on the desk. They'll help him sleep when he goes home."

Jill moved into my peripheral vision just enough for me to see that she had more than one candidate for going to sleep. She had the face of an avenger: ugly at first look but even uglier beneath that. It must have been the numbness from the injection that stopped me from feeling the same way. A broken finger—*if* it was broken—shouldn't have evened things.

Colbert came out of her haze. If a dead husband and a phony shrink splattering himself through a skylight hadn't done it for her, nothing would have. She might have bad dreams for a while until little by little, they began to fade away with the encouragement of her new romance with Cummings and the daily reminder that she still had the deed to her mansion and all her bank books. This was one Colbert who wouldn't have to worry about glances from the waiter during Sunday brunch.

I took the pills when I got home and went to sleep, no need for hypnosis. The next morning launched memories good, bad, and indifferent. But there would always be that hole in my mouth.

THE NAKED NIGHT

There were several reasons for an American teenager in Brooklyn to see the first Ingmar Bergman films that arrived in the United States in the 1950s. None of the reasons had to do with cinematic craft, artistic vision, or a taste for spiritual angst. The far more compelling attractions were named Harriet Andersson, Maj-Britt Nilsson, and Anita Bjork. Titles like *Illicit Interlude, Secrets of Women,* and *The Naked Night* didn't hurt, either. In short, Bergman was *skin.* With these early efforts, he might very well have been dipping a toe into the waters of the existential exasperations that would wash over him more maturely later on, but that was immaterial. More to the point was Andersson's *Monika* dipping her whole foot (along with all the rest of her) into a moonlit lake.

As far as I was concerned, those first Bergman films weren't even Swedish. They were simply foreign, qualifying them for one of the four Brooklyn art houses (four more than exist now) then showing European productions. There were three ways you knew they were art houses. First of all, they were about half the size of the RKO chain outlet a block away. Secondly, their marquees carried only titles, the presumption being that few patrons would be drawn by actors with too many vowels or weird arrangements of consonants in their names. The third tip-off was the posters in front of the theater that invariably depicted a glowering hero and a bare-shouldered, rueful heroine. To judge by the posters, European men never had anything to smile about, and European women were resigned to never being clothed enough for the next cold snap.

It didn't take a passport to enter one of these houses, but it might as well have. In contrast to the brightly lighted lobbies and Willy Wonka variety of treats to be found at the refreshment stands of the chain theaters, establishments like the Plaza and the Bell specialized in dusty boxes of Good 'N Plenty inside which the white and pink licorice capsules seemed to have made some chemical dye trade with one another. They weren't good, and one was plenty. Only the Plaza offered popcorn; sort of. Rather than scoop into a large glass container to fill up a bag, the parolee entrusted with popcorn sales was usually content to point a gnarled finger to a machine at the back of the orchestra and to ask whether you had enough nickels for the house's self-service popper. The nickels were the least of the drawbacks to this system. Because the popper stood directly behind the last orchestra row, motivating it into action depended completely on the glare from the screen; i.e., too many consecutive night scenes meant coins all over the ratty carpet. Even with a good shimmer from the screen, there was the problem of grabbing one of the small bags placed atop the popper, cupping it under the dispenser, dropping in the coin, and then watching as either four solitary kernels dropped down or vast fields of Iowa produce erupted over bag, hands, and machine. A couple of whirls at this, and even Good 'N Plenty's speckled whites and faded pinks started to look better.

The Plaza's popcorn machine had an impact on Bergman, too. When it wasn't spewing its contents over the floor, prompting loud melancholy ad-libs from the fool with the nickels, it was churning, grinding, or whining about its contents on its own, this in direct competition to the pains unfolding on the screen. This usually brought shouts from the 10 or 15 patrons scattered around the orchestra to the effect that they couldn't listen in peace to the language they didn't understand and were seriously considering demanding their francs back. I never saw anybody go so far as to carry out the threat (if only because the promised nude scenes from the posters had yet to come), but on one occasion, the manager felt enough pressure to unplug the popper behind some snarling about how "you don't have to hear what the hell they're saying, just read the subtitles!" I never discovered whether the man had worked previously in a library, was unable to grasp the essentials of the cinema experience, or simply had a piece of the popcorn action.

In case you didn't already know you weren't about to see a Gregory Peck western, the Brooklyn art houses betrayed their exhibition policy with their coming attractions. Instead of the usual frantic explosions, kisses, and pratfalls in rainbow colors, there was a somber black-and-white legend informing the audience that next week's film had won awards at the Cannes, Berlin, and Lusaka festivals and had been praised by whoever-these-people-were-supposed-to-be writing in whatever-these-periodicals-were-supposed-to-be. Actual scenes from the coming films were rarely shown, apparently on the theory that anything said in French or German would have been Greek to the audience being counted on to return. I always found these image-less trailers vaguely unsettling, and not only because they didn't follow the Hollywood pattern of throwing together a movie's most dramatic scenes, cutting away from them before their climax, and then splashing the big red word INCREDIBLE over the screen. What could be truly eery was the *silence*—the festival designations and critical excerpts being flashed out with nothing more than the low hum of the projector as accompaniment. It was an arrogant kind of quiet as if we were to understand that prestige was the topic here, so shut up and prepare to be as impressed as that reviewer for the Glasgow *Herald* had been.

I guess I was hard to impress. More often than not, the tradeoff for a glimpse of a bare breast was French films about Citroens driving around Paris and cops blowing smoke into one another's faces while they endlessly interrogated a suspect; German films about motorcycles tooling around Frankfurt and hookers and cops blowing smoke into one another's faces while they all modeled long black raincoats; and Swedish films about carts rumbling through the countryside and teenagers blowing smoke into one another's faces while they fenced around getting it on. The United States might have had MGM and Paramount, but Europe clearly had Gitanes and Mercedes-Benz. Beyond that awareness? Well, I had come to recognize a slew of European performers and could feel superior in my cinematic knowledge when they occasionally popped up in Hollywood productions. And granted, there was a mood about even the dreariest Italian or Swedish picture that seemed to have escaped California filmmakers—something personal, something quirky, something, yes, *sensual.* Marlon Brando wouldn't have seemed so exceptional in these settings. Barbara Stanwyck wouldn't have had to rely on incessant repartee to convey her message. James Stewart wouldn't have had to climb to the ledge of a bell tower to suggest the vertigos of daily life. Maybe that distinction should have been enough of an education for me. But it wasn't. Appreciating sensuality and appreciating the wonders of Clearasil can be fairly incompatible preoccupations.

Then I saw *The Naked Night.*

And immediately saw it again.

My first reaction to the Bergman fable about a traveling carnival troupe was annoyance. Unlike other pictures he had shot in black and white, this one seemed to have been photographed in black and white and still more white. With a perverse sense of purpose, the director and the subtitle writer had teamed up to ensure that just about every line of translation had been placed over a white shirt, a white dress, or a white horizon. Only the weary trudging of the nags pulling the carnival wagons seemed to preclude the action moving eventually to Lapland. Particularly impossible was an early sequence (presented as a story within the story) about a carnival clown going to get his exhibitionist wife away from a detachment of sex-starved soldiers. To accomplish this, the white-togged clown hurried toward a white sky, saw his white-skinned wife splashing in the sea with white-skinned soldiers, clambered down some white rocks to retrieve her, and, after realizing that her clothes had been stolen as a prank, carried her Cavalry-like over his shoulder down lime-white paths back to their wagon. The most legible lines during all this were those imposed over the wife's blonde hair.

And already, to me at least, it didn't matter. The story of the clown and his wife had enkindled one visual fire after another. The entire sequence evoked those silent Russian epics in which every close-up signified HISTORY or REVOLUTION—except this was only about a cuckold trying to get his wife to stop embarrassing both of them. Substitute smeared, sepulchral makeup for bruises and the clown carrying the wife back to the carnival camp was Brando staggering back to work in the last scene of *On the Waterfront*—except that this was humiliation demonstrating love rather than the need for a new pier boss. And when the tale was concluded, the wagon driver telling it kept rolling along a hilltop last seen in the stark imagination of Carl Dreyer—except that the only stakes interesting him and his listener, as they both emphasized, weren't those that had held Joan of Arc or that might have been used against Vampyr, but the ones needed to keep the big tent down on their next stop-off. How else to say it, but that *The Naked Night* suddenly excited me because, its picaresque carnival premise notwithstanding, it appeared to want to be about something *small*.

I had seen small movies before, of course; some of them had even been from Hollywood. But the marriage of large references to intimate drama flabbergasted me. It was neither the roar of Genghis Khan leading the Golden Horde in Cinemascope nor the drip of the kitchen sink genre then in vogue on both the big screen and television. Naive as it sounded even to myself under the spitting popper behind me, I had the enthralling thought that maybe this Swede believes we all carry our epics within us and that they don't have to end in shouting at one another about who was at fault for our shotgun marriage, tiny apartment next to the railroad tracks, and gambling debts with the bookie living over the pub.

And then *The Naked Night* scored its second hit. Normally, one enthralling thought was good enough for me to tune out of everything that immediately followed. Why risk having one's intellectual bliss contradicted too fast? Instead, though, I sank even deeper into the picture, and with bizarre confidence that I wouldn't contradict myself because Bergman was not about to contradict *him*self. Helping this self-assurance along (for both of us, I assumed) was the fact that the central drama—the growing stresses between the carnival owner Albert (Ake Groenberg) and his mistress, the troupe's much younger bareback rider (Harriet Andersson)— amounted to a macroscopic version of the clown story. There were no soldiers, but there were plenty of humiliations—the owner at the end of his rope financially, the owner promising to give up his itinerant ways and (unsuccessfully) begging an ex-wife to take him back, and the owner discovering that his mistress has slept with an actor for a worthless bauble. Then for good measure, there was the very dandified actor beating up the burly Albert in the center ring of the tent before a mocking crowd. Forget the enthralling thoughts about small, big, and epic. The picture also happened to be the ultimate teenager's manual on the romanticism of self-pity.

I've wondered more than once over the years what another screenwriter-director would have done once he had established the abjectness of the carnival owner. We know what Josef von Sternberg did with a similar type in *The Blue Angel*—no escape. We know what Mauritz Stiller did in *The Atonement of Gosta Berling*—fantasy. We can also guess at what Hollywood censors would have insisted any American filmmaker do—have Albert shoot, strangle, or drown the mistress, burn to death in the middle of a fire that destroys the entire carnival and have his ex-wife deliver a eulogy around the theme that he had always been a traveling man and was now just traveling on to another world. As ludicrous as this last option might have been, it didn't seem altogether out of the question when the hopeless Albert dug out a gun and, in between guzzlings from a brandy bottle in his wagon, pointed it first in the direction of the entrapped bareback rider and then at the clown whose earlier related humiliation he found it easy to blame for triggering his own.

But Bergman and I hadn't come so far for that kind of pat melodrama. The first clue came in the woman's hilarious lie that she had agreed to have sex with the actor in exchange for a glass trinket only because he had locked her in his room and she didn't want to be late for that evening's performance under the big tent. There was no way *that* kind of baldness could be eliminated from the planet. As transparently mendacious as she was, she deserved all the years ahead of her to perfect, grow out of, or laugh at her act. So sullenly innocent, she couldn't even qualify under Albert's slobbering lament to the clown (the second clue) that "you should shoot everyone you're sorry for." She had a lot more reason to feel sorry for him than vice versa.

So better the clown should go down? The gun-wielding owner thought about it, and the equally tipsy clown didn't seem all that opposed to the principle, but then Albert spoiled that alternative with the blurt that "I like people." That I recall, no other Bergman character has ever made such a flat declaration; for sure, I've never heard any Hollywood character say it, exception made for political windbags or con artists softening up their victims. In the Plaza that day, it seemed like such a startling pronouncement in the circumstances that I immediately claimed authorship of it. At the very least, I told myself, I was the only one in the orchestra who had been able to read the dialogue over the owner's shirt. One way or another, for what must have been two-and-a-half seconds, it seemed important to have title to that sentiment as a discovery from more than oratory, celebration, or self-congratulation.

Since Albert didn't count himself among the people he liked in general or in particular, however, that still left one dramatic option for his state of mind and for the theatrical rule about never introducing a gun into the proceedings without using it. And sure enough, he then pointed the pistol at his own temple. I sympathized with his despair: Had Bergman brought us all this distance merely to illustrate those perennial United Nations statistics showing Sweden as one of the world's busiest suicide gardens? Maybe the mistress had been ahead of the game after all with her bauble. At least she hadn't made his mistake of overpricing the moment.

But no, not to worry. Having the owner kill himself or aborting his own dramatic situation hadn't been Bergman's only remaining options at all. There had been a third one—growing from both Albert's desperate rage and the breeding of "I like people." So Albert staggered out of his wagon and, with the entire troupe stumbling after him, went over to a cage with an ailing bear that had been kept alive only because even the most rundown carnivals needed some kind of bear to sell tickets. And there Albert fired all his misery into a creature even more humiliated than he was.

I didn't dare move. If somebody had made the mistake of choosing that moment to shuffle into a seat in my row, he would have had to climb over my head. The flushes came more rapidly than the grindings from the popper behind me. Something about Humanity with a capital H. Something about this Bergman guy skipping over continents and oceans to land in the Plaza Theater on Flatbush Avenue in Brooklyn. Something about teaching all the John Waynes of my emotions how a gun could truly be useful. Something about Albert, the bareback rider, and the clown knowing more about *The Greatest Show on Earth* than the Ringling brothers could ever imagine.

The picture needed an ending, so there was one. In the last scene, in the most naked night of their lives, Albert and the bareback rider. exchange silent glances, then trudge off together behind one of the wagons toward another town. I liked thinking they knew I was waiting for them—sitting in the Plaza as the film started again.

INSTANT CULTURE

Nobody ever said culture was easy. On the one hand, historical, ethnic, and social markers declare that she is this and he that and that they are more prone to doing this thing than that other thing. On the second hand, the markers get mixed together so much over time and space that they must struggle to maintain visibility. On the third hand, this struggle precipitates superficial senses of identity that, in the best cases, underwrite annual block parties and banquets and, in the worst cases, wars and genocides. On the fourth hand, there is that belated awareness, sometimes proud, at times remorseful, that all the sweat is unnecessary, that culture simply codifies what is, capital letters really neither here nor there.

But on the fifth hand, culture is also like sex—in accounting for where our ancestors came from, it diagrams character, measures satisfaction and disappointment, and even as it binds, never totally loses sight of the *more*. The more may or may not be exotic, but it suggests the other, when not the further. Capital letters might be neither here nor there, but they insist on tickling fancies of where those places might be, how different they might be.

There is safety in thinking of the more as the different, a little like visiting a zoo and taking in big cats, bears, and reptiles within their locked confines: We can learn, maybe not experience but learn, just passing by on our own feet. We can't actually prove that anything different is worth knowing about. Who has ever truly and credibly seen a UFO and detailed what we are missing? On the sixth hand, though, are we truly and credibly so arrogant as to hold that we are the one and only species in the cosmos? Need we cling to ignorance as a belief?

Christmas seemed like the ideal time to find out. Too old for toys and too young for a yacht, I was happy to accept the envelope in between and set out for Times Square for a full day of cultural shopping. The first destination was the Capitol, where *Alexander the Great* had just opened. Insofar as Alex had been a subject of history class recently, there was academic virtue in assigning him first place in the lineup. Who knew how much extra credit might be gained from something Richard Burton blurted between B.C. duels?

The extra credit had to be earned. For the best part of an hour, there was considerable prattle about whether Philip II (Fredric March) was really Alex's father or whether his mother (Danielle Darrieux) had grown impatient in the bedroom while her husband had been off on his conquests. This soap opera in togas ended only when Burton was old enough to despise his father for marrying somebody younger than his mother, leading to all kinds of separate cliques that battle scenes of taking over more and more of the globe did little to overwhelm. The gossip that Alex was a bastard kept everybody on edge with the gods even as the maps of the world were being redrawn. Moral: Not just the super-rich, but super-conquerors had as many problems as beggars. It was a mishmash of loyalties and betrayals, never clearer than when an Alex lieutenant killed Philip for him and was swiftly executed for such well-intentioned treachery.

If there was a dominant theme to all the hissy fits, it was Alex's motto that he would rather have a short life of glory than a long life of obscurity. I sympathized and had a feeling I wasn't the only one in the orchestra who did. By the time he worked up to accepting himself as a demigod, I was thinking of all those Superman and Batman villains who indulged in similar fantasies. How else could it have ended but with a POW and a BAM? He was 23 when the POW came.

Leaving the Capitol wasn't exactly leaving Greece. A Hollywood budget notwithstanding, it wasn't leaving America, either, since March was the only non-European in the cast of thousands, accent on Burton and other natives of the British Isles. In retrospect, anyway, I had gained more knowledge of the value of Stanley Baker, Harry Andrews, Barry Jones, and Peter Cushing to international productions than of whatever Aristotle had counseled Alex. For sure, *Alexander the Great* failed to provide a conversational opening with Homer Papadopoulos the next time I dropped by his diner. It would be English muffins and leave it at that.

A few blocks south of the Capitol and about a millennium later was the Criterion and the second great conqueror of the good old days—Temujin, or as he was to be known more popularly, Genghis Khan. There were good things and bad things about *The Conqueror.* One of the good things was that it was among the first features that came with Stereophonic sound so that, unlike the periodically comatose *Alexander the Great,* its massive scenes of battle all but stampeded charging steeds into your lap. One bad thing was that the Criterion hadn't been outfitted for Stereophonic sound so that all the massive battle scenes not merely stampeded the charging steeds into your lap but sadistically into your ear canals, awakening nostalgia for Macedonian decorum.

Another bad thing about *The Conqueror* was that the lead role was played by John Wayne using a false staccato to (presumably) sound like a Mongol. Yet another bad thing was that the Tatar princess he kidnapped was played by Susan Hayward, whose milk-white skin and fiery red hair had to have made her conspicuous in her old Brooklyn Tatar community. A good thing was the orchestra hilarity when Wayne told Hayward, "You are beautiful in your wrath," and when he seemed to confuse her ethnicity with uncooked chopped meat. A bad thing was that all the actors playing good and bad Asians (Lee Van Cleef, Thomas Gomez, John Hoyt, Ted de Corsia, William Conrad) were far too familiar from gangster films or westerns or both. They, too, were directed to deliver lines like elevator operators announcing the floor coming next.

The history offered by *The Conqueror* for extra credit in school was useless. The closest it came was in the relations between Temujin and his brother Janukha (Pedro Armendariz). Historically, they fielded armies against each other for a good part of their lives, Temujin ended up executing Janukha's followers, and Janukha asked to be killed with them as long as his blood wouldn't be spilled. *The Conqueror* presented all this as a simple misunderstanding by Temujin of personal betrayal and Janukha's adamance that he be killed anyway so that no lingering mistrust between the brothers would compromise a Mongol conquest of the world. Fact met fiction when Temujin honored the request not to spill Janukha's blood by having his brother's back broken. Colorful and ugly, but no extra credit.

Across the street from the Criterion, some three centuries along, was the Victoria's screening of *Lucrezia Borgia.* It might not have had the battle scenes of *Alexander the Great* or *The Conqueror*, but it more than made up for it by having Martine Carol, the French equivalent of Marilyn Monroe, in one plunging neckline and diaphanous gown after another. She might not have been a demigod, but she was the daughter of a pope (Alexander VI), a wife or lover who was said to have had as many as ten children, and the consort of men who either disappeared from various courts only to have their bodies show up on far shores or were bought off by her father in the interests of more profitable unions. Most of the killings were attributed to Alexander and Lucrezia's older brother Cesare (a tireless Pedro Armendariz), but the picture's cardinal interest was not so much in history as in the target audience that was implied by the title it flaunted in theaters after the Victoria—*The Sins of Lucrezia Borgia.* Not that this overlooked the cultural versatility all over Times Square: Just as *Alexander the Great* had accounted for all European nationalities *except* Greeks and *The Conqueror* had decided that cowboy and gangster bad guys made for ideal Mongols, *Lucrezia Borgia* personified its royal intrigues in proto-Italy with French actress Carol and the Mexican actor Armendariz. For history, *Lucrezia Borgia* was satisfied emulating Carol by dipping its toes in the bath water and leaving most of the rest to the imagination.

Three centuries later and three blocks south of the Victoria, at the Paramount, Alan Ladd and Charles Bronson were sort of shining a light on the Modoc uprising in California in the 1860s-1870s in *Drum Beat.* The cultural conversion here was in the Lithuanian Bronson (Buchinsky) portraying Kintpuash, the Modoc chief known as Captain Jack, but the Hollywood studios had not been discomfited by whites playing Native Americans since the glaciers had melted to reveal southern California. Also, as with the epics laid in Macedonia, Mongolia, and Italy, the tone of

Drum Beat was melancholy in the wake of betrayal and reprisal violence. As a peace keeper, Ladd understood why double-dealing by the United States with the Modocs exhausted their patience and led to one shootout after another; as the earnest chief seeking an iota of sincerity from Army negotiators, Bronson understood why killing a general during peace talks would have lethal consequences for him too. Ladd understood Bronson, and Bronson understood Ladd right up to the latter's hanging as a war criminal (the only one so branded in the long history of wars with Indians).

Whether Macedonians, Mongols, or Modocs, it appeared, a lot of understanding went into graves with a lot of corpses. Was it because of the fidgety consciences of filmmakers concerned about having been too cavalier in distorting their subject matter, retiring to melancholy as a substitute for sympathy? Not likely. That would have shaded the primary cultural statement made by *Alexander the Great*, *The Conqueror*, *Lucrezia Borgia* (with or without her sins), and *Drum Beat*—that they all called Times Square their home and that commercial culture could be negotiated for a paid admission.

Some of the real cost of that enterprise did not become plain for some years until it was revealed that 91 of the 250 people who were involved with *The Conqueror*, including Wayne, Hayward, Armendariz (who killed himself when given his prognosis), and director Dick Powell died of cancers assumed brought on by the shooting of the picture in Utah, downwind from Nevada nuclear tests. Producer Howard Hughes was so certain of the connection that he pulled the picture from circulation for years. But Hughes also projected it over and over in his melancholy seclusion. He thought of it as a genuine American undertaking.

WARLOCK SCHOOL

When I was a kid, the world wasn't divided into cowboys and Indians, cops and robbers, or the United States and the Soviet Union. Far more critical was the hostile gap between plastic figurines that had bases and those that didn't. The ones with bases might have looked good on a shelf, but they simply didn't have the action potential of those without stands. How could you have a fist fight between a cop and a robber glued to underpinnings? To fall over at the end of a left hook, the pieces had to defy gravity. And once they were down, they looked positively silly with bases sticking up in the air!

Not that I had many alternatives. The pro-base lobby has always been potent among plastic figurine lovers, and the collectibles industry has hardly weakened it. My first suspicions about the ubiquity of the bases centered around my mother: that she favored toys that preened on a windowsill rather than littered the floor in some amorphous heap. They helped foster the illusion of orderly children, not to mention that this made for less bending over. As it turned out, however, it was my mother who bought me a birthday gift that drove every last based figurine into submission. Moreover, it started me down the road to a years-long addiction, provided me with a reliable test of my memory faculties, and helped make the argument that some toys are at their best when they're broken.

The gift was 12 boxed Louis Marx figurines—six mounted cowboys and six mounted Indians. The riders (two inches high) and the horses (three inches long) were separate components, and some of the riders fit more comfortably into their saddles than others. This suggested one of two possibilities back at the Marx factory: haphazard coordination between the rider conveyor belt and the horse conveyor belt or some distractions among the warehouse boxers.

Artistically, the horses had it all over their riders. They came in black, white, palomino, and roan, had the front left hoof lifted in the classic frozen moment, and carried an expression of one part elegance and one part loco weed. Most important of all, they stood freely, no need for any stinkin' bases. The cowboys and Indians couldn't stand on their own? Too bad. That's why the horses were there. Get mounted and move out.

For the most part, the riders looked like survivors from a Rorschach test conducted by Crayola. The cowboys—half with lariats and half with laterally extended six-shooters—managed to cover the spectrum with such combinations as green hats, yellow shirts, and black chaps, the occasional red or blue dot for variety atop variety. The relatively less splotchy Indians, all with the elaborate bone vests and massive headdresses of the Plains tribes, favored white and lime green as they brandished their tomahawks and lances. Face detail was minimal when not surreal. The eyes were particularly slapdash, suggesting sightless prisoners of some mad scientist's dungeon. Assuming that it wasn't just a case of some dye vat overflowing, a couple of Marx's colorists also apparently had a jovial time matching noses to Stetson and bonnet tints.

As any ten-year-old will tell you, one problem with six cowboys and six Indians is that this hardly adds up to a great battle, especially when half the cowboys hold lariats and half the Indians ceremonial lances. Fortunately, somebody in my family (no names) stepped on one of the cowboys, eliminating his rope and leaving a bare fist. This automatically qualified him for more scenarios than those having to do with cattle or wild horses, and specifically for saloon fights. I will deny to this day that I deliberately broke the lariats of the other ropers; let's just say that when they found themselves in tussles, they went at it with particular energy.

My second epiphany was discovering that three stores in my neighborhood sold similar plastic pieces individually; in fact, in addition to the cowboys and Indians, they also had cavalrymen on identical horses. To make a long obsession short, I spent the next few years channeling comic book and movie money into these discoveries so that I ultimately ended up with more than two hundred riders and an equal number of mounts. Every once in a while, a purchase would be too hasty—a horse with a superfluous node of hoof plastic that made it impossible to stand up freely, a cowboy with a very breakable leg. But very few of them had to be put down as bad buys. As soon as I got them home, they were given a starring role in a new game, complete with name and general characteristics. Without knowing it at the time, that gave me a step up on college geology courses where the major objective was to train the memory with all those genera and phyla categories. Who needed that when you were already good at identifying Slade, Flint, and Mitch out of heaps and heaps of plastic? The only problem was coming up with a plot that would justify cluttering my bedroom floor in place of doing homework. I was a lot better at leading my riders under the radiator than having dramatic reasons for doing so. It was with great relief, therefore, that the movie house around the corner started showing *Warlock*. If I couldn't come up with a credible plot, maybe Hollywood could do it for me.

The prospects were tingling. The coming attractions promised one of those expansive 20th Century Fox Cinemascope westerns where the color kidnapped the spectrum, the music score zigzagged back and forth from a Dmitri Tiomkin rip-off of Mussorgsky to a different Tiomkin rip-off of Mussorgsky, and the horses had a lot to snort about. The movie house marquee sagged from stars Richard Widmark, Henry Fonda, and Anthony Quinn. Who would be the hero, the last one standing in the street? The movie had as many possible heroes as my toy closet. Expectations were clotted to the box office ticket.

The first mystery resolved was that of the title—not indicative of a place with sorcerous traditions, merely the name of a western frontier town picked out of a hat; Tombstone and Dodge City had already been taken, so that had apparently left only Warlock. And why tinker with a classic setup such as an iron-handed mine owner whose idea of good times was to let his gunmen rampage down Warlock's main street whenever they felt like it? I had used that setup every time I had decided a scowling black and red Blackie or the deep tan Bull hadn't seen enough action on the floor. Only the fact that I didn't have the appropriate pieces prevented them from killing women and children. What I had never done, however, was to give the role of the mine owner to Bob—a sickly thin white figurine who had his hands cupped over in front of him. Bob was okay when he was on his horse and seeming to reach for the pommel of his saddle but off his horse, he looked like he was afraid of being kicked in the balls, this restricting a villainous personality. I couldn't help thinking of how inappropriate Bob would have been because *Warlock* had given the role of the mine owner not to a Robert Ryan or Lee J. Cobb but to an actor most recognizable as the boy next door in a perpetual swoon over Judy Garland. Have yourself a merry Christmas??!! Have one yourself. Where were Widmark, Fonda, and Quinn?

Granted, this casting bothered me more than it ought to have. I was sure not a single other patron in the orchestra was as irritated by it as I was. But I was there to learn, to master intricacies beyond punches in the face on my bed springs, and this actor choice struck me as a kind of unlearning. I also couldn't forget the dictum about villains being the most interesting Western characters because they did what heroes were seldom accused of—think. No question, their thinking was mostly scheming, but that trumped prattling on about the law all the time. Exception made for neurotic James Stewart protagonists; a Western heavy was more intriguing because he *wanted* something, whether gold, land, or somebody's wife. But *Warlock's* bad guy was Bob, who wanted to listen to Judy Garland sing? He wasn't the man I loved.

Fonda and Quinn finally arrived as gunmen brought in by town elders who decided that the killing of an aging sheriff was the mine owner going too far. By then, we also knew Widmark was an ambivalent townie who didn't like that his brother worked for Bob. I knew right away that the brother's death would be an excuse for Widmark's Hamlet to get over his ambivalence, it was certainly how I would have plotted out things. Brothers didn't show up in westerns unless they were there to be killed, and if that triggered a moral awakening, so much the better. I abided Widmark's stuttering until he could see his brother's corpse, vow vengeance, and get to it.

But first, we had to get used to Fonda and Quinn not as saviors but as new bad guys mainly interested in profiting from how Bob had reduced

Warlock. For a while, I thought that was great because it made for more chaotic fist fights all over my bed and floor; i.e., first, yellow Reno could wrestle with rose Rudy, then the two of them could team up against black Bart. The free-for-alls I had always plotted were being endorsed by the most major of Hollywood studios with the biggest names! For sure, all Fonda was interested in was opening up a casino and making moves on the women he hired to work in it. Much creepier and giving me some hesitation, though, was partner Quinn, a brute from Grunts 'Re Us with a club foot and scary panting hero-worship of Fonda that should have had the town elders looking into another mental asylum for their hirelings. I had a doubt or two that anything out of a Louis Marx box could deal with these complexities.

I should have had three or four. Faster than the blackjack tables in Fonda's casino were filling his pockets, various movies broke out. They brought to mind an English class in which the teacher demonstrated how to diagram a subordinate clause that modified an equally intrusive subordinate clause, resulting in a blackboard with so many jagged lines that the overall picture was a field of half-completed swastikas. One movie sufficient for an hour on the floor was Quinn hearing that the brother of one of Fonda's past victims was on his way to Warlock to even the score. No surprise about the brother's intention since that was what brothers did before they were shot down. More surprising was that Quinn neglected to mention this to Fonda and rode out to kill the brother before he could reach Warlock. The biggest surprise of all, though, was that Bob's men were blamed for the killing, and Fonda, still in the dark about how he had been protected, brought Bob's innocents in for a murder trial. Throughout all this, Quinn did a lot of smirking as subtle as his club foot.

I had no firm position on subtlety, as long as it didn't go too far. There was just so much double-meaning Abbott and Costello wiliness you could have two cement-faced plastic cowboys swap as a prelude to having them smack each other around. But I needed more than my Peanut Chews to savor the goings-on when one of the Bob gang brought in for the trial was Widmark's brother, and everybody in the courtroom shifted eyes back and forth like those tiny silver balls rolling around in search of the right hole in a patience game. What clarified matters—for a few seconds anyway—was Bob reminding the cowed jurors who he was so that his men were acquitted of the killing. The orchestra included, they were the only ones.

I conceded to the notion of the acquitted gunmen out to get even with Fonda for locking them up for something they hadn't done. Once I accepted that, I couldn't protest too much that one of the acquitted was Widmark's brother, meaning we were about to have more brother angst. And on cue, Widmark was stepping out into the street trying to talk his brother and his friends out of doing something stupid. Naturally, they did something stupid and were killed in a duel by Fonda and Quinn. And then the fourth and fifth movies started.

I was as vulnerable as a Hollywood studio head to the demands of actors. If I had several favorite figurines in some scenario, I made sure each had a spotlight moment or two. Throw in the thousands of dollars required for a Widmark, Fonda, and Quinn, and I understood how the screen time demands in *Warlock* were more imposing than those in my bedroom. I wasn't naive. I grasped how the business world worked.

Nevertheless, a mess was a mess, and the Peanut Chews in my hand couldn't compensate for it. It was surely an omen that the two mounds I had left were beginning to melt in their wrapper. When things start to melt in the middle of an orchestra, you can't just unmelt them.

As though they hadn't already done enough, the town elders realized that their cure of Fonda and Quinn was worse than the disease of Bob, so they asked Widmark to take over as sheriff. Just as he was about to fall back into ambivalence, he was assaulted by Bob's henchmen and had his gun hand broken for having failed to back his brother in the duel with Fonda and Quinn. I didn't know how to explain that turn of events to the boys in the closet. Forget Abbott and Costello, I needed a Chinese playwright in the original Mandarin. To whom did Widmark owe loyalty at this point? And how did I make a convincing argument for it to Louis Marx's boys? My confusion got so depressing that I wanted just to leave all the figurines on the floor so somebody would come in to sweep them into the garbage, cleaning up Warlock once and for all. A passing thought, unworthy of the hours of joy and instruction that had gone into the figurine scenarios, but still a thought. And, of course, there was worse to come.

Widmark might have had his broken hand, but Quinn suddenly had a broken world. First, there was Fonda's interest in a woman, to the point that he talked about retiring as the wandering gunman, marrying and settling down on a farm, a ranch, a sawmill, or wherever else emotionally exhausted gunmen settled. Something about Quinn's grunts said that he loathed the woman part even more than the settling part, and he implored Fonda to move on with him to some new town needing gunmen and a casino. For practical reasons, I could see some of his argument: The only women figurines in my bedroom were three breastless Annie Oakleys hoisting their Stetsons above their curly blonde hair and clasped tightly into bareback horses for some acrobatic bullseyes. No way they would have appealed to a deliberative Fonda, let alone to a psychotic Quinn. Did the guys lined along Louis Marx's conveyor belt hate women as much as Quinn? I hadn't posed the question before, but the answer appeared to be yes. Bases were bad enough. Suppose, though, the real underpinning for the Marx collection was Quinn's clubfoot mentality? I didn't like that possibility. It seemed to make me smaller, too.

But women weren't Quinn's only problem. He had hated the idea of the town elders appointing Widmark the town lawman. He hated it even more when Widmark, his broken hand and all, told Bob that he had shot up Warlock for the last time, and Bob had come riding in with a few henchmen anyway. Quinn already had his hero at hand, and it wasn't Widmark so that when Fonda announced he was going down to the street to help the sheriff, Quinn disarmed him and locked him in his hotel room. There was no way he was going to be a party to making that sheriff more of a hero, especially through the assistance of his own hero. I couldn't imagine things getting more warped, not where heroes were concerned and in light of imminent events that came down to meaning that I simply couldn't imagine.

Bad hand and all, Widmsek faced down Bob and a few of his roughnecks. It seemed like years since the main problem with Bob had been his fixation on Judy Garland; now, it was why he was still keeping the film projectionist busy. For once, the town elders did more than act like town elders, blowing away Bob's men and leaving the mine owner to Widmark. Down Bob went, up went Widmark as a true Warlock hero.

Except from the casino window where Quinn had watched everything, realizing that keeping Fonda out of things had backfired on him. Nobody was going to leave it at that. Not me because I would have still had too many characters spread out around my floor with little sense of justice acquitted. Not the projectionist since he knew how many reels had yet to be unspooled. Not Quinn because he had too much invested in his personal object of hero worship. And not Fonda because he finally recognized the seriously disturbed man he had as a partner and knew he should have been guilty about a few things. Quinn declaring he was going down the street to kill Widmark was his moral cue.

Or something.

Sometimes I had bored even myself by repeating a fisticuff action; when Joe jumped off the pillow a second time to unhorse Latigo, I knew I had run out of story and probably should have been getting to History homework. On another day, I might have been comforted to think of million-dollar productions running out of originality as much as I did. I might have yielded to another reassurance that the projectionist had mistakenly put a used reel back on his machine. But it wasn't another day. It was the day I had dropped in to enliven my imagination, and the more *Warlock* went on, the less primitive my Louis Marx good guys and bad guys seemed to be. They didn't need help from Hollywood. If anything, Hollywood needed them. When I looked more carefully, even the Crayola colors of my figurines were more eye-catching than those that had been splashed over the Cinemascope screen. And I hadn't spent a fraction of 20th Century Fox's money in my neighborhood stores. Did that make me the modest one?

You had to be there to believe it. I was. Playing a minimal variation on how Quinn had locked him in his hotel room, Fonda closed Widmark into a cell so Quinn couldn't get at him. Widmark didn't understand, but that was all right because I did. When Fonda was the one to walk out of the sheriff's office, Quinn didn't understand. But that was all right because I did. That might have ended it right then and there, but then the jeers from onlookers about how he feared Fonda gave Quinn pause to do more of that stupid. He fell dead to Fonda's bullet in the same patch of street as the old sheriff, Widmark's brother, and Bob and his men had. Cemeteries accommodated fewer bodies than that piece of real estate in Warlock did.

After all these massacres, it was time for feeling. I remembered it from the day I had devised an especially long story with green Tex discovering that burgundy Mac had been his father after a fatal duel in front of my floor-length closet mirror. I hadn't been sure when it was over whether it should have ended that way, and I had been a little slow about gathering up the pieces and tossing them in the toy closet, and going out to supper. Eating had felt somehow hasty that night. I didn't have to explain that to Fonda. Quinn had been an out-of-control pervert, but he had also been his partner. Partners weren't supposed to kill partners; brothers all right, but not partners.

On the other hand, they could give them glorious burials. Fonda didn't have a Viking ship handy, but he had his casino. After stretching Quinn's body out on a gaming table, he burned down the whole place, deaf to some townie cries that a good breeze might turn all of Warlock a little too crisp. By now, it had become clear Fonda would have been the most morose of catches for any woman on a farm, ranch, or sawmill. In light of his fire zone concerns, he also remained a threat to what remained of the Warlock community. No great surprise, therefore, when Widmark ordered him out of town by the following morning. Fonda shrugged off the ultimatum, saying he would leave when he felt like it.

The first thought, of course, was about how the circle was (finally) going to be closed with the showdown between Widmark and Fonda. But the second thought was more bothersome, at least for me. To wit, there was all that Hollywood studio money on display, including that for Cinemascope dimensions that could have encompassed entire states in the frame, but for more than two hours, most of the action had been concentrated within an area comparable to that between my bedroom radiator and clothes closet. Big was small, really only a distraction. You had to be one of the town elders to be intimidated by it. And even they had finally found the courage to help Widmark against Bob's henchmen. In short, the next moral cue was aimed at me, and I wasn't quite sure why.

Morning broke over Warlock as it habitually did—with two gunmen facing one another in the chunk of street turned duel pit. Widmark went for his gun only to see Fonda's already pointed at him. Fonda finally had something to smile about before holstering his superiority, mounting his horse, and riding away from Warlock. Widmark's expression of grateful admiration said that was just as well before he succeeded Quinn when it came to the objects for hero worship.

Some endings were more definitive than others. When I rode home to my bedroom from Warlock, I sensed the Louis Marx gang in the closet already waiting in apprehension. Their equality to the characters in *Warlock* also made them somehow lesser, and we all knew it. More imagination was required, and base or no base, it couldn't be the plastic kind.

THE SEDUCERS

It was the Italian director Michelangelo Antonioni who brought Joe Brenner and me together. I was in a Broadway luncheonette talking with a friend about how sensual Antonioni had made his love scenes between Monica Vitti and Alain Delon in *The Eclipse* when a sharp-faced man with wavy gray hair and frameless glasses suddenly leaned over from the next booth and asked me to repeat what I had been saying. Within seconds of hearing again our ever-so-sophisticated theories about the differences between the sexual and the sensual, Brenner was inviting my friend and me to accompany him to a screening room to help evaluate some police melodrama he was thinking about buying. Since it was either see his free movie or drink more watery coffee, we went along.

The picture turned out to be an endless grainy exercise, apparently shot in a busy airplane hangar. For the most part, two paunchy community theater actors sat around as cops in a squad room bitching about their frigid wives, leering to each other at reminders of past encounters with hookers, and daydreaming about these oafish conquests. Whenever a blurrier than normal lens announced a flashback to a striptease or a bedroom scene, Brenner sat up in his seat and muttered, "Now let's see if this one is sexual or sensual." By the time the projection was over, he had decided not to buy the picture because, notwithstanding the fact that he had never actually seen an Antonioni film, it didn't have "any of that Italian guy's touch."

What might have been merely an anecdote for the afternoon became a few dollars when I was asked to clear my calendar the following day for another screening, this time for a Danish picture Brenner had "heard good things about." Returning to the screening room the next day, I was introduced to a surly character named Porter, who was then directing what Brenner referred to as "my biggest production right now." Porter clearly thought he had more important things to do than watch seduction scenes from Danish movies, and while Brenner was conferring in the booth with the projectionist, sneaked in a couple of zingers about "all this European crap" and the people who fell for it. The screening room lights dimmed, and Brenner stepped back inside to say: "We're going to cut right to the screwing scenes. The radio's saying something about Kennedy being shot. Now watch this and tell me why it's so sensual."

It's absolutely true everyone remembers in detail where they were on November 22, 1963. I was watching the seduction scenes from the Danish feature *A Stranger Knocks* in a Ninth Avenue screening room, then earnestly debating their exploitation value with Brenner ("That's exactly what I'm looking for!") and Porter ("Give me that Dane's money and I'll do better shit in my sleep!"). Even more vividly, I recall the elevator ride down to the street. By then, John Kennedy had died in Dallas, and, floor by floor, stunned workers in the building entered the car to get a breath of air downstairs. Feeling the need to break the gathering pall around him, Brenner nudged Porter in the arm, asking aloud: "You know Abraham Lincoln was a Jew?" Deep in his own thoughts about how to pocket some Danish kroner, Porter just shook his head, saying no, he had never heard that. "Oh, yeah, he was shot in the temple, wasn't he?" All these years later, I remain convinced that only some overwhelming impotence—a group dread of endless disabling shocks—saved Brenner from having at least one pair of hands wrapped around his throat.

In his own field, though, Joe Brenner had the genius to match Antonioni's. Rather than wait for dubbed European trash to wash up in New York harbor, he made regular trips to London to scout the British B-movie scene. "You pay a few more bucks for an English picture than a French or German one," he explained, "but you make most of that back by saving on dubbing. Sometimes you even get something that makes sense."

Not that Brenner entertained serious hopes of discovering a feature already suitable for his market; his more modest target was a picture that would lend itself to insertion work without much expense. The ideal case was the project he was then working on with Porter. Originally, the movie was a humdrum British tale about a gang that robs a bank and makes off with the attractive teller as a hostage. Back at the gang's hideout, all the standard types emerge: the leader who isn't so bad after all, the goon who wants to rape the hostage, the young punk who wants to kill the hostage and take over the gang, etc. What made Brenner reach for his wallet to buy U.S. rights were two scenes in the melodrama. In the first one, the gang leader rescues the teller from the goon, throws her into the bedroom where she is being held, turns off the light, and locks the door against any further attacks. In the second one, the leader and the teller realize they love one another, exchange a tepid kiss, accidentally knock over a lamp, and freeze in fear that they've been overheard by the ambitious punk.

For Brenner, the key to both scenes was the light being extinguished. This enabled him to cut into the action, hire a local actor and actress who in the darkness might (with great audience imagination) be the British players, and add soft-core, naked gropings. These were the scenes Porter was directing in a photo studio near the Garment District.

At least part of the time. What else Porter was doing was inviting a succession of cronies to the photo studio to show he was an unappreciated Alfred Hitchcock. In drafting me as a special production liaison between him and Porter, Brenner was livid he had to think twice about what should have been a two-day shoot, but what had, in fact, already run into a second week. Or, in his words: "What the hell's he shooting over there—*Lawrence of Arabia*?"

Porter wouldn't have laughed at the comparison. When he wasn't telling the actor playing the gang leader-in-the-dark that he couldn't act or complaining that the actress playing the teller-in-the-dark needed to go on a diet, he was ushering visiting friends over to his viewfinder so they could admire his angles on the flophouse cot that was standing in for the room where the hostage was being held. "Know where I learned that?" he was prone to asking his groupies. "From Pudovkin, the great

Russian director! We were in a film unit together during the war, and he showed me things Hollywood still can't do! What you're seeing there is the same framing he used in *Mother*!"

Brenner might not have known who Vsevolod Pudovkin was, but he didn't have to think twice about who the mother was. When Porter began demanding "10 or 12 extras" for a nightclub striptease scene that he suddenly deemed essential for beefing up the British sequences of the Scotland Yard manhunt for the bank robbers, creative differences between the front office and the set reached critical mass. Then, after a couple of days of threatened walkouts by Porter ("The day I need Joe Brenner to make a living I go into a different craft!") and threatened firings by Brenner ("I walk over to the Port Authority, I find a Porter coming off every bus!"), there was a compromise—the soundman and me. Porter had won his point about the striptease insert, but Brenner wasn't about to pay a dozen extras, even if they figured to be the dealers, hookers, and drifters he had scooped up from 42nd Street at $10 a head for his other productions. Instead, he announced like Cecil B. De Mille, revealing his solution to the Red Sea sequence in *The Ten Commandments*, the soundman and I would hold glasses of iced tea at a cafe table and project leers at the stripper. And with that, it was a wrap.

For a few months, Brenner phoned to set up more screening room consultations on that elusive sensuality. The closest he came to it was acquiring the distribution rights to an Ingmar Bergman import that, in between shrieks and lengthy silences over the bleakness of the human condition, showed some naked actresses going at one another. But both of us also had a moment of glory from our most serious collaboration. Mine came the day I was passing the Rialto theater and was dismayed to see my leer at the stripper blown up to Godzilla proportions on posters around the box office. The downside to this, I realized instantly, was that I would have to keep my parents away from Times Square for the foreseeable future. The upside, of course, was that I was able to boast to actor friends that I had reached Broadway before they had.

Brenner's success was the kind he valued most—financial. Apparently, in the interests of filling up space, a weekly magazine sent a clown of a reviewer to see the bank heist film that had taken on the new title of

The Seducers. The reviewer was so taken with the professional production and the competent acting (the original British cast included Shakespearian veteran Kenneth Haigh as the gang leader, "Man from UNCLE" and "NCIS" co-star David McCallum as the homicidal punk, and then-Mrs. McCallum and the future Mrs. Charles Bronson, Jill Ireland, as the teller) that he urged his readers to be less hasty about condemning the quality of 42nd Street soft-core releases. His only reservations, he said, were about a couple of unnecessary sex scenes and a nightclub striptease. Thanks to that review and campy follow-ups by other periodicals, *The Seducers* went out across the country billed above the most recent Cannes Film Festival winner.

"It's a great business, isn't it?" Brenner laughed. "I'd never leave Times Square."

Ultimately, though, he was left—first by hardcore pornography and then by a new Disneyland. The sexuality was pretty easy to recognize, the sensuality not so much.

CAPRICORN THREE

Reality tests can be crude. Like the time I was in the back seat of a car listening to a published poet upfront rhapsodizing about how life was only a figment of the imagination, what we called reality an illusion. The driver, a non-poet who had been making occasional sounds to indicate he had been doing something like listening, suddenly lifted both hands from the steering wheel, sending the car moping toward a guardrail. Crying out to God, Baal, and whoever else presided over Long Island highways, the poet grabbed for the wheel until, after maybe a moment of observation too long, the driver took it back behind the snicker of snickers: "I thought reality was only an illusion," he said.

Crude. Nowhere near as argued as some refutations of philosophical tracts, artistic speculations, and special delivery letters from hallucinogens brandishing similar notions. And not ventured to the fullest, who could say if a guardrail only *seemed* like a guardrail and was merely a projection from another dimension? Nevertheless, as was the case that day in the back seat, my empathy has always been with the snicker.

I could claim a supermarket shopping list of reasons for that point of view. One is that I'm just obtuse, woefully bereft of the far stretches of mental vibrations. Another is that, whether secure or smug, I simply want this world to be it and have no incentive for interpreting the corner street sign for Main Street as a "Twilight Zone" passage to the Universe Without a Name. I don't think it's incidental that I find stories dependent on such ploys boring, and not only because they provide writers with a built-in *deus ex machina.*

I have some schooled reasons, as well, for snickering. More than one person I've encountered who shares the poet's whimsy (alert: editorial opinion) has confessed to being an atheist or agnostic, so is it outlandish to conclude that for many, the reality-as-an-illusion sentiment is compensation for the absence of a St. Peter at the heavenly gates and lusty virgins behind it, a secular *other*? On a more emotionally fraught level, as popularized by the likes of Monty Python cartoons, there is human existence as insect life awaiting a shoe to come down on it; i.e., unable to see the forest because of the trees. And as a corollary to that apprehension, there are obstacles from reality-as-illusion to that most basic of all human needs—self-importance. Surrender that, surrender everything. Forget the distant galaxy species able to recite the United States capitals in the alphabetical order of their last letters before we manage to recite the alphabet itself. Reality-as-illusion isn't about humiliating comparisons with interplanetary creatures with enormous heads, more limbs than a giant squid, and admirable grades in SATs; it's about us and only us and whether we truly believe the us is us as only we could love an us. Self-importance has only one self. This one, thank you.

Admittedly, belief in ourselves alone is tautological in the extreme. Mirrors can't be trusted to show more than our appearances; after all, they have been made in this realm. More admittedly, not even what had been an imminent appointment with a Long Island highway guardrail changed my poet's perspective on all things real and might have been real. Years later, he was still churning out verse that made the least of earthly travails. Had he had some personal experience having nothing to do with drugs or orgasms or symphonic *crescendi* that had solidified his convictions? It didn't help that like the children at Fatima and Lourdes who had seen the Virgin, his answer on this point always (and only) contained some variation on "Isn't it obvious?" The secular had indeed never seemed so religious.

What all this has to do with Mars began being forged the day I dropped into a Times Square movie house to see *Capricorn One*, the thriller about how far Washington might go to have the world believe the United States was the first to reach that distant planet. Serendipity put me in an aisle seat behind another aisle seat that was unoccupied— sort of. In fact, the seat in front of me was being governed from the adjoining spot by a black fire hydrant of a man I soon came to know as Harry. If Harry's companion had gone off for popcorn edgy about losing her seat while gone, she had seriously underestimated him. No sooner had a caricature of a Brooks Brothers ad from his tie knot to his briefcase come along with his eyes on the space than Harry gave him the kind of thumb wedge last used cocking the hammer of a .38. Junior Exec knew better than to question the traffic signal and beat it in the dark to another section. Harry shook his head in wonder before the innocence of the human race.

Things weren't much better on the screen. The ceremonies of the blastoff to Mars had barely ended when the three-man crew was whisked out of the rocket ship and, miraculously unseen by the TV cameras of half the world, flown to a hangar in a desert landscape. The three astronauts were mystified, and this was even before O.J. Simpson became more associated with murder and robbery, James Brolin more famous for being the father of Josh and husband of a pop singer, and Sam Waterston devoted to two lifetimes of "Law and Order." The man with the explanations was Hal Holbrook, a NASA bureaucrat who reported that defective somethings in the something of the rocket capsule would have doomed the astronauts before they got beyond Cincinnati, so it was decided to abort things—sort of—to avoid negative publicity. In compensation, the hangar had been fitted out as a Martian TV set from which they would send reports of their mission (wink, wink). A computer facsimile would do the rest. Such a colossal ruse was in the interests of national security; they had to understand.

The astronauts might have, but Harry didn't. "Bullsheet," he growled, drawing out every letter to sound like an eastern European wrestling with English. "Who believes that bullsheet?"

He didn't get the chance to elaborate on his critique because just then, a scrawny woman in a beret and raincoat and makeup like cement on her face plopped down on the empty aisle seat. Instead of a bin of popcorn, she had two twenty-dollar bills in her hand that she practically slapped into Harry's chest. He evidently knew her since he barely looked at her as he grabbed the bills with one hand and reached into an inside jacket pocket with the other. What he found might have been grass or might have been oregano, but the beret lady seemed sure enough of her connection that she took the packet without hesitation, stood up, and returned the aisle seat to its unoccupied status. Harry had to stomp his foot at the absurdity of what was going on. "You tellin' me they're makin' a plane hangar Mars?" he asked nobody in particular, and especially a couple two rows down annoyed by the commentary. "I may turn my place into fuckin' Venus!"

The astronauts were skeptical, too. At first, they played along with Holbrook's plan, sending love messages to their wives and children and assuring the world their mission was proceeding perfectly. But then their consciences started acting up. Harry wasn't surprised. "Oh, oh, no way this don't end up like sheet," he warned them and everybody else sitting in the orchestra. "Get the hell outta there!"

But it was too late. More crossed wires in the computer facsimile popped up, and this time they fried the astronauts to death—sort of.

"I told the assholes, didn't I?" Harry's question was to the next occupant of the aisle seat, a bruiser who might have left his furniture van double-parked outside the movie house. He was certainly in no mood for conversation about *Capricorn One*. "I even had to pay the admission to get in here," he complained in his version of a whisper. "So I don't need another stickup with you."

"When did Harry ever fuck you over?"

"There's always a first time. What you got?"

"Love and kisses, baby," Harry said, reaching into his jeans pocket and coming out with a packet twice the size of what he had given the beret lady. "I like three figures. What do you like?"

The bruiser sighed; he had been here before. "You're really pushing it, man."

"Yes or no?"

There was nothing indecisive about Holbrook's look when he was told about the newest snafu. With a complicit congressman, his logic was impeccable. "We can't have them showing up if they died all over the world. I'll take care of it."

Brolin and the others had figured as much, so they agreed to separate into three directions to increase the chances of getting out of the desert and telling the world what had been going on. And they weren't alone. A journalist (Elliot Gould) had begun sniffing around after a friend working on the Mars project had tipped him off that something was amiss. The bad news was that the friend was soon scrubbed from the planet. The worse news was that the reporter was knocked around by the police and Federal goons sent by Holbrook and then fired from his paper. "That motherfucker better find a new line of work," Harry advised gravely.

But Gould didn't, following up scant clues that led him to Brolin's wife (Brenda Vaccaro) and the suspicion she might have received a coded message during the TV transmissions that there was something wrong. This made her develop a new detachment toward Holbrook, who told her that a state funeral would be held for Brolin and the other (not-so-dead) astronauts. The government sympathized.

The kid in the NYU windbreaker resented the competition from the screen for Harry's attention. "C'mon, man," he pleaded. "I can't sit here all day."

Harry nodded to himself to see that Simpson was the first one tracked down by Holbrook's military killers. "Never a white one to go first. They put a Chinaman in there, and you have some suspense. But no Chinaman."

For somebody anxious to get out of his seat and start the rest of his day, the windbreaker had a lot of reservations about the packet Harry handed him. If he could have seen any better in the darkness, he might have examined each shred of grass individually. "Doesn't look right," he temporized.

"So forget it. Adios, muchacho."

"I didn't say . . ."

"That's good. People here want to enjoy the movie."

A woman on the other side of the aisle peered over for a closer look at so much chutzpah. She had a point, of course. I also wondered how much Harry had laid out to keep cops and ushers and other uniforms away. The only thing missing was a plaque on the aisle seat in front of me for memorializing the location for the transactions.

The windbreaker gave up his resistance more readily than Waterston, who sought escape by climbing a cliffside that might have come from Dover only to find more military killers waiting for him at the top. For Holbrook, that left only one plausible direction for finding Brolin, so he unleashed his men there. And none too soon because Gould had found the hangar for Mars II and was starting to figure out that one and one added up to three.

Harry's next customer needed only a baton with his sweeping white hair, white silk shirt, and mourning coat. An affected British accent had apparently ceased amusing Harry a few deals back. "I'm busy, Count. No bullsheet."

"Three joints. Ten dollars. Right here."

"I look like the Five-and-Dime to you?"

It was a trial for the Count to repeat himself, but he somehow managed it. The effort was wasted in any case because Harry had stopped jumping back and forth to the screen with Gould's inspiration. On a bet that the missing astronauts had to be lost somewhere out in the desert, he found a crop-dusting pilot to scout with him. Harry gasped to see that the pilot was Telly Savalas. "Holy shit, baby! It's Kojak!"

"All right. Two joints."

But Harry was higher than he would have been smoking everything in his pockets. "That's Kojak, baby! Say goodnight to the mother fuckers."

The Count didn't go that far, but he didn't object, either, indulging Harry's diversion in the apparent hope it would be of help to his negotiating. Eyes frozen on the screen, Harry might have been a two-year-old exposed to his first cartoon. When Savalas and Gould spotted Brolin inside an abandoned gas station and threatened by two helicopters of military killers, they taxied down a roadway until the astronaut jumped into the plane with them. The helicopters pursued, prompting a lengthy ballet with the crop duster, machine guns up against pesticide. Finally, Kojak suckered the helicopters toward a mountainside, emptied what pesticide was left in the tank, and pulled up just as the helicopters lost direction in the clouds and slammed their way to death.

Harry was beside himself. If the lights had been up, he would have stood to cull applause from the house for a climax he had seen coming from the first appearance of Savalas. What followed elsewhere was anticlimactic. Gould and Brolin made it to the funeral just as Holbrook was looking reverential about burying the astronauts. Vaccaro had to give back her widow's weeds. The Count went off with a single joint, Harry making it clear that even that much was sheer charity for the crumpled bill he received in return. Last seen, Harry was smoothing out the bill to even it with the others he had collected during the movie and in preparation for the next show.

No denying it: I had a feeling of deep disappointment in walking out of the theater to the illusion of honking cars and an ambulance siren.

KIND HEARTS AND CORONETS

"He looks just like the other guy," my father said, and he was right. It was the fourth or fifth character Alec Guinness was playing in *Kind Hearts and Coronets*, and the sound from the living room easy chair was of someone beginning to suspect he had been pickpocketed.

What you had to understand was that my father watched movies about as often as he watched the sun rise—only from sleeplessness. He liked cracking that the last time he had been in a movie house, they had hit him up for a donation for fighting polio. He didn't hate the movies. He wasn't one of those fanatics who thought they were bad for your morals or your eyesight. They just weren't any more a part of his world than Indonesian food was. But here he was this rainy Saturday afternoon with me, not only watching a movie on TV, but one that was 70 years old, in black and white, and English! More than that, he had been the one to stop my finger on the zapper while I had been looking for an out-of-town ballgame. "Hold on a second," he had said. "See this one?"

I had been so dismayed by the sudden interest in his eyes that I hadn't told him I'd seen the thing in whole or parts maybe a hundred times. "It's funny," I had said, deciding on some half-truth that might have gotten me more than seeing the Texas Rangers take on the Kansas City Royals. "But I haven't seen it in years."

Since he hadn't objected, hadn't even thrown in one of his usual watch-what-you-wants when I visited, I had put down the zapper and let the various Alec Guinnesses perform for him. Here and there, I had thrown in a laugh in what was at most a smile moment, but at least once that had gotten him to teethe a laugh, too. Now, though, he was beginning to observe Guinness's impersonations more warily. "They make this after the Second World War?" he asked.

"Not too long after, yeah."

He nodded. "That explains it. The Brits were broke back then. Only thing they ate was kidneys because that's all they could afford. Figured it was cheaper to hire this one guy instead of paying a whole bunch of actors."

"No, he did it all the time. That was part of the comedy."

"Sure. And the guys who made this, they're laughing because they have to pay only one guy for all these parts."

"That really wasn't the idea."

"I'm not saying I wouldn't do the same thing in their place. The Brits were destroyed by the war. No money anywhere. Had to economize where you could."

"But Alec Guinness, the one doing all the parts, he was known for doing things like this."

"His union must've loved that!"

"I don't think they objected."

"Sounds like a great union."

"Everybody thought it was funnier this way."

"What's funny about a couple of guys not getting work?"

"Nothing, Dad."

"Try something like that over here and the unions would have the studio closed tighter than a drum."

"Yeah, maybe."

"Then you tell me. When did any American actor try to get away with this kind of thing?"

"Can't think of any."

"Damn right. Unions here have always been more serious. Imagine some Jimmy Stewart or Paul Newman playing ten parts. They belong to a union, too. There'd be hell to pay. But you had the war and the economic problems for the Brits, so the unions gave them a pass."

The grunt said the English would always be beyond him, and so would I for making their case. Then Guinness came on again, this time as some ancient noblewoman, and my father squinted in recognition. "This guy does them all!" he exclaimed. "He play the living room chair, too?"

Not as humorously as some other people, I thought.

THE WORLD'S GREATEST SINNER

With rare exceptions, the religious pieties of the immigrant Jews who operated the motion picture industry for decades were not directed to synagogues but rather to the Catholic churches around the corner. In part, this was because of the iron grip Joseph Breen and Catholic lobby groups such as the Legion of Decency had on the Motion Picture Code and the liberty of a film to get from a studio to a neighborhood cinema. Related to that was an emphasis on the fervid promoted even in secular arenas during the Depression, World War II, and the Cold War. Related to almost everything was the convenience of priest and nun characters for avoiding the Code's *bete noire* of sex. Little surprise, therefore, that among those donning a collar or veil on the screen were Bing Crosby, Spencer Tracy, Ingrid Bergman, Henry Fonda, Charles Boyer, Frank Sinatra, Claudette Colbert, William Holden, Gregory Peck, Loretta Young, Dana Andrews, and Rosalind Russell, and that was without the stray non-corporeal angel as played by the likes of a Cary Grant or those gaining redemption (James Cagney, John Wayne, Marlon Brando) through a priest. Even iconic tough guys such as Humphrey Bogart, Edward G. Robinson, and Robert Mitchum, who portrayed Catholic religious figures only as a disguise to elude pursuers, were worn down by their robes and cassocks to mend their ways. The very least of it was *The Song of Bernadette* and *The Miracle of Our Lady of Fatima*.

It wasn't a one-way street, either. At mid-century, numerous Catholic universities were exploring film programs that the most candid of them admitted had as an objective increasing a Catholic presence in the industry. This militant aim might not have led to any kind of religious putsch in Hollywood; there were too many competing economic and artistic priorities for that, but it helped to provide the industry with a fortifying infrastructure that went beyond the traditional trinity of production, distribution, and exhibition and that encouraged everything from independent film schools to a higher social profiling often involving even the government. The movies were *serious*, not just a weekend or tabloid diversion, and the serious filmgoer did not relax his moral or intellectual standards to attend them. (And on the off-chance that he did, there was always a regressive prelate such as Francis Cardinal Spellman of the New York Archdiocese to remind him of the hellfire he was playing with.)

Individually, many actors wanted the public to know that their Catholic yearnings didn't start and stop with the role in a script, taking part in radio and television shows that equated their faith with their talent and success. Little of that seemed to bother producers who were otherwise allergic to sectarianisms that might threaten box office receipts. Only in the gradual, then not so gradual, passing of the torch in the Sixties did the social frames of reference of the studios become as irrelevant as their executives. But not everybody was up for the transition, smooth or otherwise. For some impressed enough to view the Baltimore Catechism as a potential script, there was far too much haste in abandoning those tested social schemes. Cultural assumptions so inbred both individually and institutionally could not be edited out so glibly. One actor who bridled was Timothy Carey.

Carey was one of the busiest supporting players in film and television in the Fifties and Sixties. A grim, Gothic figure at 6'4", he attracted one director after another as an off-center presence who could shake up the scenery, usually improvising lines and antics to the visible discomfort of fellow actors. The director who gave him his biggest boost was Stanley Kubrick, who cast him in *The Killing* as a goofy marksman who kills a horse during a race to divert attention from a heist and then as a French soldier arbitrarily selected to be executed to cover a military debacle in *Paths of Glory*. But it was also Kubrick who had to fire Carey during *Paths of Glory* when the actor became so obsessed with gaining personal publicity that he engineered a story about having been kidnapped, forcing the filmmaker to use a double for some key sequences. Despite such episodes, Carey continued to tease big-name directors, working as one of Marlon Brando's henchmen in *One-Eyed Jacks*, turning down Francis Ford Coppola for "Luca Brassi" in *The Godfather*, and having Quentin Tarantino dedicate *Reservoir Dogs* to him. By his death in the 1990s, he had become something of a midnight movie cult figure, even appearing on the album jacket for *Sgt. Pepper's Lonely Hearts Club Band.*

But in case anyone hadn't noticed, Carey had never been satisfied following the direction of others as an actor. He also thought of himself as a director and a writer, and the Kubricks, Brandos, and Coppolas, to say nothing of the journeymen with whom he worked in endless B pictures and on television, had done nothing to blunt those ambitions. As he told one reporter, he had enough material from his own life to be an entire movie production, starting with the fact that his parents had once been associated with Al Capone.

Carey himself, though, responded to other associations. Growing up in Bay Ridge in the rock-and-roll era that preceded John Travolta and disco, he knew long before he had a story for putting around it that this music would have a central part in a project. Another element would be the nine-to-five routines that had always baffled him as a foundation for middle-class living in residential Brooklyn. But most of all, there was the Catholic upbringing that had kept him close to both the authority and the charisma of the parish priest. Priests were a star turn, and the audience didn't walk out on them. What eventually came out of these preoccupations was *The World's Greatest Sinner.*

For better, worse, and more worse, *The World's Greatest Sinner* had already been shot when Carey decided that he might have an easier time getting a distribution deal if there was some kind of support for it from the Catholic Church. He embarked on that mission with John Culkin, a one-time Jesuit teacher of mine who invited three of us to accompany him to Carey's Bay Ridge apartment one evening to hear the pitch. It wasn't easy to decipher. While his wife kept the platters and bottles coming from the kitchen and an oddly silent but smiling twenty-year-old introduced as Brendan sat listening to what he had undoubtedly heard a dozen times before, Carey launched into a monologue on arrogance, blasphemy, sacrilege, and other topics debated more frequently in a confessional. We all understood that they had to do with *The World's Greatest Sinner*, but without seeing it, no one, especially a Jesuit with some assumed connection to film distribution connections in the Church, could offer a practical reaction. Optimism was not aided when the enigmatic Brendan, continually referred to by Carey as "a great young actor no one in New York gives a chance to," finally opened his mouth for a brogue that, if the Liffey, would have left Dublin under water.

But the next day, there was a screening of *The World's Greatest Sinner* for Culkin and friends in Manhattan. Writer-director Carey starred as insurance agent Clarence Hillard, whose first appearance shows him being fired as one of the soulless nine-to-fivers because of his objections to peddling policies people didn't need. He goes home and tells his wife he is determined to create a world where life insurance will be unnecessary because all human beings will be immortal; she nods off to sleep in the middle of his diatribe. He gets more of a sympathetic hearing from his pal Alonzo, who also happens to have tickets for a rock concert. When he sees the wild enthusiasm for the rockers, Clarence decides that it will be his vehicle for gathering followers, and so he takes up guitar lessons. From that point on, the music track belongs to Frank Zappa, hired for the occasion in his pre-Mothers of Invention years.

Even in the darkness, Carey's absorption with his screen self made it clear he wasn't watching a comedy or a satire or a lampoon or any of those genres that a filmmaker has meant to be taken with a pound of salt. He took the actor, the writer, and the director more literally than that, and Timothy Carey or Clarence Hillard, mouthing lines in unison with those coming off the screen, still did. Culkin's expression said he maintained hope—maybe not for a miracle of the loaves and fishes sort but for a celluloid scrap that would make him sound earnestly critical when he informed Carey that he had limited influence with movie distributors accustomed to obeying the Vatican. In the meantime, he clutched a roll of Life Savers, seeming to implore them to deliver on what they promised.

Having somehow persuaded some Bay Ridge neighbors that they are all superhuman, Hillard faces minimal opposition in changing his first name from Clarence to God. He also forms the "Eternal Man's Party" with himself and Alonzo as its chief officers. But an initial party meeting ends in chaos when the attendees can't agree on what minority group to hate to gain more publicity leverage. Hillard has to console himself with another of the elderly widows he has been seducing for their life savings for financing his party. Alonzo, a son of two of the brightest Three Stooges, does his part by creating posters that depict Hillard as half-Jesus and half-Hitler as might be conceived by Salvador Dali. He also voices doubts, however, that some people might get the idea that Hillard aspires to be a dictator. Hillard assures him that isn't so, then organizes an extravagant concert that features stripping and cavorting with a snake. When an onlooker objects, a riot breaks out, and the Eternal Man's Party gets maximum media coverage. When an ex-follower approaches Hillard to recount how being in God's party had left him in a suicidal state. Hillard recommends that the man go home and kill himself.

"Really a sign of how degenerate he's become," Carey whispered to me.

Who wouldn't have just nodded?

Things start falling apart at home, too. His wife, oddly content with doing the laundry to that point, warns God that he has gone too far. His daughter comes home from school after being taunted for her father's notoriety. Worst of all, his mother arrives for a visit, hears what he has been up to, and accuses him of sacrilege. He tells them all to shut up, then goes off on a national tour. While on the road, he is approached by a political king maker who advises him to throw away his guitar and concentrate on running for the Presidency. Hillard doesn't have to be asked twice, and he is soon kissing every woman in sight, including one girl barely into puberty.

"Another sign of how low God has fallen," Carey whispered, no irony around the word God.

Culkin glanced at me to say either that he hadn't heard, had heard but would have preferred not to have, or had never understood why there were so many lemon flavors in a Life Savers roll. He turned his eyes back to the screen as if for a punishment he had coming.

After causing so many crises for others, Hillard has one of his own when he is told his mother has died. And all his promises of immortality? He couldn't get it even for his own mother? His most zealous followers decide he has been more talk than faith and accuse him of being an atheist. He withdraws from the scene for a moment of private grief, leaving it to Alonzo to come up with a spin for placating the zealots. Alonzo's notion of a spin is a tornado when he declares that Hillard is the one, only, and true God. Hillard doesn't reject his crony's vote of confidence, precipitating yet another crisis in demands that his wife stop going to church to pray to what he now considers a rival. When his daughter demands he swear on the Bible that he is still a Christian, he slaps her, and that is finally enough for his wife and the kids to leave home.

Hillard decides on a showdown with that other entity claiming to be God. He sneaks into a church and steals a Communion wafer from the tabernacle. As he hurries home with it, he doesn't notice the demonic slime he is leaving on the ground. Once home, he takes a pin and sticks it into the wafer, daring it to bleed to show that it is the symbol of god as proclaimed by Catholic doctrine. When it merely crumbles, he exults as the one and only true god. But as he leaves his house, blood trails after him. He is frozen in the final credits as he realizes there is a more genuine god than God Hillard.

It didn't take a week for the lights to come up in the screening room; it just seemed that long. The first retreat was to the blood in the final sequence—Carey proud of how he had introduced its gory color in the otherwise black-and-white picture, Culkin nodding that he had indeed seen it and thought it clever. Then instead of the previous talk about blasphemy and sacrilege, there was the more laic consideration of egomania, megalomania, mass hysteria, Nazis, and various penal code clauses. Culkin couldn't have agreed more: all elements touched on. Then, not to try the patience of the elephant in the room any further, he noted that *The World's Greatest Sinner* could hardly be regarded as holiday fare for parish halls. No argument there, Carey quickly agreed; all those sex scenes with the widows and the young girl, not exactly *Going My Way.* Though some could be toned down. And the suggestiveness of the snake—the picture wouldn't really suffer if that was eliminated altogether. But the important thing, he was sure Culkin had to agree, was that the picture stressed the importance of true religious devotion, no false gods tolerated. If Culkin had the time, maybe he could suggest scenes that might be trimmed for heading off objections.

Culkin didn't have the time or the vocabulary. In a confessional, he usually had sins to focus on for granting absolution; only occasionally did he have to propose the razing of an entire life with its every implicit and explicit attitude. Who—*what*—was to blame for such a warped idea of faith? He didn't know Bay Ridge, Brooklyn well enough to figure it out, but he would give it thought and be in touch. Carey said fine. Carey was an actor.

The World's Greatest Sinner went on to two lives. The first was industry scorn that embraced even Zappa in calling it "the world's worst picture" and telling numerous interviewers that the cast had been recruited from "Skid Row." The second, years after Carey had been waked and buried, brought out all those who would have disturbed him more than the College of Cardinals—those sure the picture was deliberately camp, that it was an acidic commentary on all those who took religion, politics, music, insurance policies, and just about anything else seriously. A popular word on social media was masterpiece, as in Bach and Michelangelo.

Leaving the screening room that day, Culkin recalled that in *Going My Way,* Bing Crosby had worn the cap of the St. Louis Browns. "They don't exist anymore," he reminded not altogether unhappily.

LONELY ARE THE BRAVE

If there is a legendary American figure more popular than the cowboy, it is the vanishing cowboy. This is not too surprising. While historians at the onset of the twentieth century were proclaiming the closing of the western frontier, militarists in and out of uniform were busy herding foreign peoples on distant shores rather than cattle on a Texas trail. National melancholy glazed international expansion. The cowboy, facing demise, assumed the character of collateral damage, overwhelmed by new social forces that he had to cope with alone on horseback. This supplied the reverential distance for the romanticism of the equally overwhelmed living in cities but pursuing less exposed ways of life. For them, the deer and the antelope might have still been playing out on the range. Ambition was the next camping site. What a simpler life than their own! Who needed trolley cars?

What the before and after romanticism had covered over, of course, was that a cowboy's life had, for the most part, been a grubby existence for the next job, the next drive, the next dollar. Except in rare cases, he wasn't the one who saved his money and bought the Ponderosa; if he was lucky, he would draw close to that owner so as to be hired and sent to a cot in the bunkhouse. The comforting reading for this daily struggle was of the cowboy's *independence*, and the cowboy himself was not averse to such an emphasis. Self-delusion can be a saddle sore, too.

The first time I went West, I had a few sores of my own. I wasn't looking for stray heifers, just for some kind of sense as to why my wife and I had married too young and now had decided on a separation even younger. San Francisco wasn't the Chisholm Trail, but its mild coffee cake air held out the promise of tasty breakfasts before taking on the horizons of the day. And for a while, the promise seemed on the verge of developing into a little more. There were some old friends, then a couple of new ones. There were temp jobs weeks long and others hours long, but paying what their verbal or written contracts had stipulated. No one was getting rich. No one was gaining a new professional passion, but no one was getting cheated, either.

Sometimes a dime-store glamor was thrown in, such as when an actor friend talked me into getting up at dawn to go with him down to Market Street to a casting call for the movie *Once Upon a Thief.* When we got to Market Street, we found enough people lined up for a remake of *Ben Hur.* My friend wanted to line up; I told him I wasn't an actor and strolled off to Fisherman's Wharf, where lo and behold they were shooting an actual scene for *Once Upon a Thief* with Ann Margret, Alain Delon, and Van Heflin. More lo and behold, someone tapped me on the shoulder and asked whether I would be an extra for a couple of shots. It wasn't a Brando character, but it was show business.

Irregular as they were, incidents of the kind made for a tempting confidence jauntiness. New as the city was to me, I was sure I could navigate streets I had never walked along before. Give or take a hill or two, asphalt was asphalt. Parks were parks. Experience was experience. I hadn't left the sun back east. It was still overhead, watching out for me. It *knew* me.

The reality interludes were every four or five days on the phone calls with my wife. Where she was, the traffic lights at our corner were still changing from red to green, the same music was on the same radio station between news bulletins and weather forecasts, and she was wondering if we had any better idea of how much longer the separation should go on. There were so many possibilities that every one of them felt inadequate.

Minus co-starring with Ann Margret, it went on like that for a couple of months. It would have been nice to blame mood swings on changes in the weather, but in San Francisco, that was as credible as attributing weather changes to mood swings. I might have paid more attention to how routine the drizzly fog could be, but who trusted cheap omens? On the other hand, it was certainly a bad sign when I began defect hunting. I had heard his anecdote before. I didn't like the way she came close to spitting when she exhaled her Chesterfield. Was he bent on putting Mennen deodorant out of business? Wouldn't San Francisco have been livelier on the Atlantic? And why all the gentility anyway? Was I supposed to forget there had once been a Barbary Coast where men had been shanghaied for crews? Imperfection and hypocrisy wherever you looked!

The TWA ticket was a compromise between the check I sent east and my wife's account. No one was conceding the slightest; both parties of the both part were still at a gauging stage. That also left two days to say goodbye to people I had barely said hello to and catch a movie on Market Street. The movie was *Lonely Are the Brave*, and I refused to read some sarcastic message in the title. As I said, I was no fan of cheap omens.

Lonely Are the Brave was what they called a modern western, meaning both sexes wore Stetsons to drive pickup trucks. But the protagonist Jack Burns (Kirk Douglas) stuck to his horse, which got spooked near automobiles and had to be kept away from busy highways. I wasn't Spartacus so that I could take or leave Douglas, but only a few minutes into things, I sensed this might be a taking time. He was one of those vanishing cowboys, and with a vengeance—didn't carry a driver's license or any other ID, a pleasant smile for anybody who couldn't understand his indifference to what presumed authority had to say. Not a beatnik, hippie, or any of those other tribes grouped by the epoch, he was just Jack Burns who relied on his instincts to see him through the day. As romanticized loners went, he defined the species.

When we meet Jack, he is stopping off at the ranch of an old friend in New Mexico. There he learns from the friend's wife (Gena Rowlands) that her husband has been arrested for helping to smuggle Mexicans into the country. At this point, *Lonely Are the Brave* layers its narrative—what is said explicitly between characters and what Jack is silently plotting to do next. There is no doubt that even as the dialogue underlines that he and his friend's wife have had more than one fantasy about one another, he remains preoccupied with how to break his friend out of jail. She knows it and doesn't like her ambivalence about it.

Jack shows his indifference to another social piety in going to a seedy bar with the intention of acting disorderly enough to get thrown into jail with his friend but runs into a disturbed one-armed veteran. Unable to avoid a fight, he puts one arm behind his back, to be fair, making him prey for the veteran's tactic of trying to strangle opponents with his empty sleeve. When Jack uses his free arm for defense, he is jumped by onlookers for assaulting a "cripple." The arrival of the police is good, bad, and worse news. Good: They're used to answering calls about the veteran and are well aware that he starts trouble. Bad: Jack doesn't want to be sent on his way because he would be failing to get to jail. Worse: He slugs one of the cops to get arrested and ends up sentenced to a year behind bars.

By then, I knew that Jack wasn't a loner who could have been played by John Wayne. He was too spontaneous about his irreverence, cared less about abstract principles like the Law or Justice than about the people mangled by them. And without a dollop of self-righteousness: He wasn't after converts, but only objectives in the here and now. Did that make him selfish? That was for the selfless to judge.

He ends up in a cell with his friend (Michael Kane). When he reveals the file he has hidden in his boot to help them escape, though, the friend says no, thanks, he intends going into court to denounce the exploitation of the Mexicans crossing the border; besides, he has a wife and home. Even more disastrously for Jack, his intervening in an attempt by one of the guards to beat up his friend earns him the beating instead. The adamance of his friend to stay in jail leaves Jack no alternative but to escape without him, his only accomplishment the one-year prison sentence. He returns to the ranch for his horse, says goodbye to the wife, and takes off for the nearby mountains.

I had felt it coming, but the dam broke with the rear angle shots of Jack loping off for the mountains. The easiest tears were for the character of Jack Burns and for how one amiable intention after another had provoked his escalating troubles. But there was more than that pressing on my chest, including my response to the movie itself. With more nerve, I would have stood up to warn the theater the picture was about to back away from Jack in favor of some Walt Disney glop. Add it up: A horse plus a cowboy plus mountains. It was even money a cougar would soon be prowling around after the horse.

What was going on, I didn't want to be told, was everything. Jack, Hollywood's cold feet when it came to genuinely rebellious characters, the TWA ticket, the compromise, the separation, the marriage. So much was suddenly *predictable* and in very slow motion, but nobody had done anything to head off any of it. The script had to be followed from the first page to the final fade out, improvisations discouraged. Jack was still affecting cool, but no one was that cool while being chased so he could be thrown back into jail for serious time. What he was doing was trying to ignore the doubts building in his head. Thank god he had to concentrate on steering his horse up the sheer mountainside. Deeper thoughts he would get to later—much later, if he was lucky.

It was all too raw: one stupidity leading to another one to a third one and on and on. Nobody deserved it, but benevolence was needed. That was the job of a sheriff (Walter Matthau) who was grumpy that his deputies failed to swat as many flies as he did in his sleepy office. He had nothing personal against flies or against Jack but went after them all anyway. As Walter Matthau, he spoke circuitously, so it gave me time to think circuitously, to measure, for example, the consequences of returning the TWA ticket—a more definitive announcement of separation than the first one. At least then, we had been at the kitchen table and seen each other's faces. From one coast to the other, it would have been all virtual, leaving the hard part to TWA and bank employees.

The sheriff's benevolence brought static. Authority veered toward the folksy—not exactly a cougar prowling for dinner but still Disney. It was a tempting distraction, needing some of Jack's grit to ignore. However easygoing, the Law was still the Law and demanded its piece of flesh. Continued resistance had to apologize to the warm and friendly, even what some considered the human. You had to be insensitive to reject the invitation, not to accept the opportunity for comforts of a predictable order. What could Jack possibly like about himself for saying no?

Surviving dangers, that was what. The first was none other than the guard who had beaten Jack in the jail. Since he knew the terrain, he picked up the trail of the fugitive faster than everyone else. He got as far as getting the horse in his rifle sights before Jack was sneaking up behind him and clouting him on the skull. Neon signs instantly flashed SATISFACTION—for the beating in the jail, for trying to kill the horse, for whatever else needed to be satisfied. But then one thought too many: Assaulting the guard would make it harder for the sheriff to maintain his benevolence.

And then it became impossible. The state police picked up Jack's whereabouts from a helicopter that zoomed in and out of his feeble attempts to hide under trees and brush. Not out of bad choices, Jack fired at the copter's rotary blades, sending the ship crashing to the ground. No way now for the sheriff to walk away benevolently. An outlaw was an outlaw, not an in-and-out-law. Commit or don't commit.

But the copter cops survived the crash, as they should have in a Disney movie. And if they were able to, Jack had to, as well. His energy was restored as he worked his way up the final yards of the mountain. Balboa setting eyes on the Pacific couldn't have been more elated than when Jack reached the top. The tears began to stir again, but only so far as my throat—a clogged feeling of triumph that brought an expiration hour with it. There was still too much hope attached to things. Triumphs should not have had hope hanging on; that stage had been in the past. But here, it still was sharing the moment with achievement. What the poets called ineffable, not to be translated into scrawny words.

I was resigned to disaster as Jack nudged his horse down from the top to claim his freedom. There was no surprise in the sleek highway running across the foot of the decline that he was negotiating. Why else did we know that his horse went crazy at the sight of traffic? Everything had been planned way ahead of time. But it was absolutely insulting that the messenger of death was not just a truck but one transporting toilets!! Sarcasm? That was effable, not ineffable.

The rest was by the numbers. The horse shied in the traffic. Jack began to lose control of the reins. The truck driver swerved to avoid a collision. Jack went helplessly toward the swerve. The driver hit the brakes too late. And then, except for pitiful whinnies, silence.

The benevolent sheriff arrived on the scene along with lots of squad cars with lights rotating on their roofs. The truck driver was devastated.

A vet was giving the horse a fatal injection. The lump being shuffled into the back of an ambulance was the still-living Jack. The benevolent sheriff was asked if it was Jack he had been pursuing. The benevolent sheriff had to shrug: he had never seen the man.

Collateral damage had that way of seeming unimportant in retrospect.

FRANCO AND CICCIO

Flavio prided himself on recognizing Americans. What gave them away, he said, were their eyes and their jackets. The eyes always looked ready to believe until they were offended by something, then they turned icy, never to return to their sympathy. The jackets were always windbreakers with a big letter on the front and the name of some university or sports team he had never heard of stitched across the back. Wasn't he right?

So Flavio wasn't a profiling specialist for the FBI. On the other hand, there was something to be said for somebody who walked up, introduced himself as the operator of a small Rome *pensione*, and instantly offered you free board and meals. Since he didn't have any real, genuine, authentic Rolex watches wrapped up and down his arms for two bucks apiece and didn't ask for a down payment on the free bed and board, I lingered long enough to hear him out. It's always that initial misstep that leads to trying to scale Everest.

With his *pensione* in the shadow of the central Stazione Termini, Flavio relied on the daily international trains as the pipeline for his boarders. His proximity to the station was an advantage in that travelers didn't have to walk far for a meal and a night's sleep for a very moderate price. But it also implied disadvantage since arrivals who gave priority to being near the station were usually only overnights, their plans already made and tickets already bought for going on to Sicily, Florence, or points further north the next morning. Such a relentless turnover made it imperative Flavio put in 10-hour days at the station. As he made immediately clear, though, not even that kind of grind had been making the *pensione* anything like profitable.

His long hours weren't his only cross. Another was the flock of hawks from the hotels and larger boarding houses who, as soon as a train pulled in, formed a gauntlet to hem in passengers trying to reach the station arcade from the track platforms. Although no more subtle than Flavio in going after the arrivals with their aggressive chants of "Room! *Camera*! *Zimmer*!", they sported little extras—caps with the names of their hotels, baggage dollies ready to assist travelers—that made them appear relatively more reputable. With his long beak of a nose, rheumy eyes, and a rash descending from his Adam's apple down into his shirt collar, Flavio was not so much a hawk as a scabby magpie—and that was before he opened his mouth to release a high-pitched squeak of a voice. Travelers who bought his pitch for lodgings were sometimes seen only in the opening sequences of horror movies.

Which was where I came in—or at least where my windbreaker did. In exchange for full board, he explained, all I had to do was accompany him to the station every day for the most popular trains and just stand there as if waiting for somebody. How could travelers fleeing the hotel hawks *not* see me as a friendly refuge for practical advice about where to find a room? Everyone knew an American when they came across one, he surely did, and I was as obvious as the Statue of Liberty. Whereupon I would earn my keep by escorting the new arrivals over to his place. No overt badgering, mind, because that would have alerted both the station cops and the hawks. I didn't want to get picked up for soliciting without a work permit and get jailed or deported, did I? I started to tell him the question had never occurred to me one way or another before running into him, but he was already on to greater danger than the police. Some of the hawks weren't nice people, he warned; they worked on a commission off the number of customers they collected and didn't need any competition from Americans. Italians had had enough of that stuff from the auto and film industries. It wasn't beyond the hawks to get physical about driving me away from the station. And that was without mentioning those who would simply point me out to the cops, getting us back to the jail time or deportation possibilities.

It was at this juncture that I asked Flavio what his name was, this usually being among the amenities when people first meet, and one of them launches into job, sleep, and meal offers. He looked duly embarrassed for having skipped that part of the introduction, but there was an even deeper glint of shame in his eyes, as though he was used to social gaffes and to having others remind him of them. Right there would have been the moment to wish him luck in his endeavors and to move on. But there was a reason for not moving on—the half-second it took to calculate the money in my pocket. Free board and meals wasn't just an offer; it was midway between a necessity and a miracle. I'd had promises from an acquaintance to slide me into a production assistant job at the Cinecitta movie studios outside Rome, but the acquaintance was long on dyspepsia and talked of Italian unions as if they were negligible obstacles in the way of his sour guarantees. Anybody who had ever heard the phrase *general strike* knew that wasn't true. I also took it as a bad sign that the gentleman of one part breeziness and forty-one parts rancor used the same description of *negligible* to measure Michelangelo Antonioni as a director compared to himself, even though he had never directed a picture in his life, had, in fact, advanced into his middle years assiduously compiling a list of enemies who had thwarted his film ambitions. In short, harebrained as it might have been, Flavio's scheme for attracting boarders shaped up as a bullet train to lucrative tomorrows compared to the cart named bile that was supposed to transport me out to Cinecitta.

The *pensione* was both bigger and smaller than I had expected. On the basis of the original blueprint, it consisted of five sprawling rooms, a spacious eat-in kitchen, and two bathrooms on the second floor of a venerable stone building guarded by a *portiere.* But having decided sometime before that this wasn't large enough for the armies he envisioned putting up, Flavio had cut up three of the rooms into eight cubicles, each of them containing a cot with a double mattress, a table with a reading lamp, two straight-backed chairs, and a free-standing plastic closet. The truly luxurious compartments also had most of the windows that had been intersected by the plywood dividers. The spaces weren't much for touch football, but they were ideal for solitaire.

If she had been in a TV series, Flavio's wife Daniela would have been an Italian Alice Kramden from *The Honeymooners*, right down to the loose curl of hair hanging off her ear. An attractive thirty-something who scraped around most of the day in bedroom slippers, she was beginning to show wear at the edges from having to entertain so many of her husband's schemes, to the point that she was as given to eye rolls as much as to speech. Being presented to her as the fulfillment of Flavio's latest vision didn't enlarge her vocabulary. A passing satellite would have picked up her clear preference for hard cash from the newest boarder.

There was one exception to the *pensione*'s overnight trade—a prune-faced journalist from Rimini who, though not yet 50, was already into his second year of retirement. This wasn't the easiest information to get out of him since his muttering foxed Flavio's Italian almost as much as my excuse for it, and drawing too close to him to hear better risked being overcome by the Vesuvius of cheap Italian cigarette smoke he spouted without letup. Obviously, the man had a great retirement plan. In the meantime, it seemed enough to know that he was Gianni, that he was on an open-ended stay that had already lasted three weeks, and that he could never pass through a room without going over to kiss Daniela's hand. Flavio seemed to think this cheap feel reflected the man's noble breeding, and with his peculiar habit of leveling his eyes slightly above the person he was addressing, Gianni was the last one to discourage that impression. Wasn't it enough he lowered his gaze and risked seeing the riffraff by kissing her hand? As for Daniela, she responded to his oafish advances depending on her mood—sometimes as the most attention, she figured to get on the day, other times as part of the tedium of running a *pensione*, and yet other times as though her hand wasn't attached to her body.

Like all good coaches, Flavio broke me into the station routine gradually, starting off at a night hour when only two important international trains had yet to arrive. I was hardly alone in my trawling. First, there was a skeleton gathering of hawks, at their customary position at the arcade gates and moaning to one another about the scarce pickings during the day that had made it necessary for them to be still on the job so late in the now faintly eerie station. Then there was a shifty character in glasses in front of a shuttered news kiosk; as he hopped up and down against the night chill, he seemed to have to force himself to focus attention on the platform where the first of the two trains, from Amsterdam, was due. He might have been a drug pusher looking for new markets, he might have been waiting for the secret nuclear plans being brought to him by someone on the train, or he might have been a cop; what he definitely wasn't was the waiting friend I was supposed to be. Whole minutes of experience made me confident of that conclusion.

Then there were the hookers. About a half-dozen of them, in uniforms of leather skirts, tight sweaters, and open-toed heels, kept coming and going from the arcade to hot sheet rooms across the street. When they weren't trying to catch the eye of disembarking passengers from the suburban trains, they kept themselves busy enough with the Romans who meandered into the station, knowing this was the place. According to Flavio, there were undercover cops around keeping an eye on them, which seemed a little like assigning a weatherman to a downpour to make sure the rain stayed wet. The most conspicuous of the so-called undercovers was one I came to call Tonio. Within 15 minutes of glancing in his direction, I had seen his belt holster twice as he slipped his hands into his pockets to hitch up his pants. Then, wearing as much leather around his brawny shoulders as she was around her mighty hips, he ambled over to the arcade bar table where an overweight hooker in an overweight red wig had been nursing an *espresso* for a half-hour. He mumbled something that came with a smile and another hitch of his pants, drew an annoyed reaction from her, then wandered along toward the exit fronting on the hot sheet rooms. She waited a minute, took a last drag on her cigarette, then got up and rumbled after him. Two of the other hookers standing nearby saw her off with disgusted laughs. That was when I saw I had probably been right the third time about my friend with the glasses in front of the kiosk: As soon as the hooker went off to give Tonio his freebie, Glasses wrote something in a notebook. He looked very cop-ish doing it. Internal Affairs keeping an eye on their own? I didn't get the answer to that one until weeks later, and from Gianni, of all people.

Flavio turned out to be a genius. Maybe not as the term was usually applied to Shakespeare or Einstein, but in his own field. The very first night, a backpacker from Omaha got off the train from Amsterdam, all but decked one of the hawks who converged on him, and spotted me as his rescuer. The following afternoon it was two English girls barely out of their teens who decided I was part of the Lend-Lease program. In both cases, so as not to alarm the curious, I made oversized gestures to cover, telling my prospects to wait across the street for me so I could lead them to the bargain of bargains. Only when the hawks had lost interest in me did I casually rejoin my customers outside. By the end of my first week, I had snagged seven boarders (two couples accounted for four of them), which together with Flavio's four made for what he glowed had been the best week in the history of the *pensione*. Granted, I might have imagined it, but for a few days, even Daniela seemed to restrict her eye rolls to Flavio's victory speeches at the dinner table. She saved her most despairing reactions for his announced desire to eventually move to a larger space and decorate the new *pensione* with American flags. "Everybody has to specialize," as he told me more than once a day. "All Americans will know that when they come to Rome, we'll be like their second home." I gave him a smile in a way I thought Daniela would have endorsed: It was supposed to come out as a wince.

But not even Flavio's meal-time jubilation could disguise his persisting problems. One was that most of our catches remained overnighters, meaning no relief from the long hours at the station. Then there was how, for all her skepticism toward the empire-building going on around her, Daniela threw the little money given to her into food splurges that would have flattered guests at first-rate hotels. This was the one benefit to having mostly overnighters and to owing them only coffee, bread, and jam for breakfast. Those who rented cubicles long enough for lunches and suppers learned that "something simple" for Daniela meant four-course meals with plenty of wine. Naturally, Gianni expected nothing less, and the bounty on the table twice a day gave him two more excuses for kissing her hand. When I mentioned to Flavio how he might—just *might*—be chasing himself around in circles financially with such extravagant meals, he only shrugged that the lunches and dinners "keep her happy, and I want her to feel part of things." Since Daniela also did the heavy cleaning in the place, I had never doubted she felt part of things, but that was as much as he was ready to discuss the subject.

The best part of thinking about Flavio's problems was not having to think about mine. Starting with the backpacker from Nebraska, the boarders who stayed for a few days assumed that when I wasn't down at the station, I was on duty as their tourist guide. The drawback to explaining how wrong they were was that it invited too many meditations on what I actually *did* do when I wasn't fishing for more customers. The best answer seemed to be drinking grappa with the neglected D.W. Griffith, who didn't think much of Italian unions. Even this diversion came to an end after the day he pulled me along to visit a painter friend on the Via Margutta. Going up the stairs to the woman's apartment, he encouraged me not to be diplomatic about what he called the "garbage" on the walls. The problem, he said, was that the painter had been putting up for months with a tenant who fancied himself an artist but was mainly just a free-loader. He had tried telling her that, but she had dismissed his views because of his naturally crabby personality. If I had the opportunity, he said, tell her what I really thought, and maybe she would realize how much of a fool she had been. Which was what Little Dorothy, without her red shoes, did. It wasn't hard. The guy who opened the apartment door looked like every caricature of a gigolo ever conceived and had never straightened out the difference between a smile and a sneer. The canvasses on the wall were as oppressively empty as D.W. had said. So when the painter asked me what I thought, I told her—in the name of love, as the song said. Too bad the art turned out to be hers, and D.W. had his nastiest laugh in months (or minutes). Bottom line: I tried to enjoy the Forum and the Colosseum with my *pensione* charges.

When I didn't have anything real to be melancholy about, Flavio was there to pick up the slack. It took a few days for me to find out about it, but it turned out I was a lover who refused to accept that the great passion of my life would stand me up in Rome. At least this was the *Waterloo Bridge* story he had fed the hawks when they began getting too inquisitive about my daily station presence. With a gift for fantasy I had detected only in his plans for the *pensione* and a talent for straight-faced lying I should have picked up on at our first meeting, he had a couple of the hawks shaking their heads in pity for the American who kept coming back every day hoping that Bette (as Flavio, a fan of Bette Davis, called her) would mend my broken heart by showing up on one of the trains from the north. One of the hookers saw her opening and advised me to forget about Bette with her. Tonio told me I was being a fool. Glasses only showed up sporadically after that first night, but I assumed he had filed a report in his notebook about Bette and me. It was never too late to kill Flavio for his fable, but once spread around the station to everyone but the track announcer, it was too late to come up with another lie.

When there was silence to fill, Flavio liked talking about us being partners one day at the new American *pensione* he had in mind. He seemed to think of the gurgling sounds I made in response as confirmation I shared his dream. Apart from his reveries over his grander *pensione*, his major lift out of the gray present came with a weekly jaunt over to the Ambra Jovinelli, a rickety movie house a few blocks away that paired Grade Z Italian features with live shows and charged prices even I could afford. He wouldn't hear of me not accompanying him when the bill changed every Monday, a slow night at the station anyway. A double-tiered hall that reeked of lilac deodorizer, the Ambra Jovinelli was one of the last of the city's showplaces dating back to the turn of the century. The cheap ticket prices helped guarantee mobs for the evening shows, the audience consisting not only of neighborhood people but of droves of soldiers waiting for their nearby train connections to postings around the country. Nobody went just to see, either. As Federico Fellini would record some years later in his *Roma*, both the variety shows and movies were interactive experiences before their time.

The tattier the shows, the more audiences loved them. A typical bill would start off with an emcee comic who was to be seen in every burlesque house from New York to Djakarta. The jokes might have been indigenous, but the comic's leers were international, and the audience's groans at the punch lines intergalactic. After the comedian came some aging Rolando in a gaucho's hat and two blondes in rhinestoned bustiers who towered over him even without their glittering spike heels and feathered tiaras. As much as the blondes had the men in the front rows slavering over their monumental thighs and plunging necklines, they had the whole house in still greater anticipation for the moment when the gaucho started swirling them around as dance partners. When they didn't throw out his back, they at least got him to spin himself into the ground. Before regaining his balance, Rolando heard an avalanche of wisecracks from the orchestra and balcony the opening act comic could have used for brightening up his routine. Nobody had the house roaring more than an act of the kind calling itself The Three Tops. The idea was that the first man would toss the blonde to the second man; the execution was that the blonde, who must have been on Daniela's "something simple" diet, sent the tosser staggering back toward the wings with his release and absolutely flattened her would-be catcher. It took The Three Tops more than a minute to overcome the audience laughter and pretend their flopping around had all been part of the act, then—for reasons beyond the plausible—go on to another number that also risked their body parts. Through it all, the hefty blonde kept her teeth gleaming and flipping her hand for the audience to applaud her winded partners as masters of acrobatic dancing. The audience did what it was told.

The showgirls weren't the only ones who had too much to show; in fact, the physically overripe was a running motif for Ambra Jovinelli acts. The juggler injected extra suspense into his number by raising the question of whether he would get all his plates past his paunch; the magician's hair and mustache had been waxed so black they looked like Halloween candy. The highlight of most bills was a singer a decade or more past a career peak. Rarely did they come on stage without being preceded by a psychedelic light show and a boomed recording of their biggest hits back when all of this geared to having the audience cheering and stomping before the much beefier or sepulchrally thinner troubadour appeared. After a ramble through the past hits, there was inevitably a closer that stunned everybody into silence—from the men some dirge about a dead mother, from the women an even more morose lament about the lover who had gone off to get married and left them to collect rags on the street. Flavio was seldom without tears in his bloodshot eyes by the time the finale ended, and the house erupted.

He had another kind of response to the movie shown between the live shows. Next to Bette Davis, nobody enthralled him more than the comedy team of Franco Franchi and Ciccio Ingrassia—to hear him tell it, anyway. Franco and Ciccio seemed to make a picture a month, all of them big on toilet bowl jokes and 200-pound women who were determined to entrap them in bras and girdles. That was the best part of Franco and Ciccio. While Ciccio was a mustached pencil who played the straight man in a Bud Abbott fashion, the seemingly double-torsoed Franco was a Jerry Lewis on steroids who defied the odds he couldn't do anything more excruciating than his endless mugging. Actually, he could—endless animal sounds emanating from a nightmare set in the world's loudest pet store.

Flavio played his part as ritualistically as the comedians played theirs. After bubbling all the way over to the theater about how Laurel and Hardy had nothing on Franco and Ciccio, he barely got through the opening credits before slipping into a deep sleep. What was there to say? Wake up, you're missing a masterpiece? The truth was, not only was the man exhausted by his daily hustlings at the station and the *pensione*, but the only company he could find for an occasional night out was an American he barely knew. For Flavio, there was no getting away except to the sleep provided by Franco and Ciccio.

I thought.

The first hint of imminent change was Flavio's indifference about going down to the station with me two days in a row; he should have had a cold or the flu, but he had neither. He went down the third day, but mainly to jaw with the hawks. It was also a little odd to hear the detachment in his voice about a warning from the undercover cop Tonio that some of the hawks had been complaining to him about me. Apparently, some of them had seen my Bette's latest apparition as Baby Jane and no longer believed I could be heartbroken that she wasn't on any of the arriving trains. For Flavio, suddenly an impartial observer to what I had been doing down at the station, it would have been unwise of me to ignore Tonio's warning; in fact, it might have been smart to stay away from the Termini altogether for a couple of days.

Then came the morning Daniela introduced me to two wrestlers as her brothers. They couldn't do more than grunt because they were busy pulling a credenza out from a wall and carrying it to the front door. When Flavio appeared from one of the cubicles with the bedding in his hands, he had the same shameful look as the first day at the station. Then he had merely forgotten to give me his name, this time, he had forgotten to mention that he and Daniela were moving in with her ailing father. But there was nothing for me to worry about. He had talked to the people who would be taking over the apartment, and they had assured him both Gianni, and I could stay for another month without having to pay rent. It would take them at least that long to tear down the cubicles and move their furniture in. I wanted to howl and bang my feet up and down about our Stars and Stripes *pensione* partnership, but then I remembered that would have been Franco Franchi's reaction. It wouldn't have been any funnier from me than from him.

Within a week, the only pieces in the apartment were the furnishings in Gianni's cubicle and mine, along with some crockery and a coffee maker Daniela had left in the kitchen. Caverns never looked so cavernous. Footsteps never sounded so intrusive. I stayed away from the place during the day as much as I could, and through the Via Margutta painter who had a sense of humor about everything except D.W. Griffith, met some people who didn't need rooms. One of them even got me a job as a translator. There *was* life in Rome outside the Stazione Termini.

It was usually very late when I went back to the gutted *pensione* for sleep and a change of clothes. But no matter the hour, I found Gianni sitting in his cubicle and reading an Italian detective novel by his weak table lamp. As soon as he heard me come in, he dropped the book and ambled over to my cubicle for another installment of his adventures in Rimini. Over time I had made some progress with his Italian, but none at all with his inaudibility. If I hadn't seen Flavio and Daniela also craning their necks to pick up something he had said, I might have taken him for a hearing test I was constantly failing. What was especially irritating was the certainty he was aware he had me and the rest of the world leaning toward him and liked it just fine that way. He really didn't want to encourage conversation any more than he wanted to look people in the eye. He was satisfied just having a pair of ears for whatever scoop he wanted to reminisce about.

The way he told it between loud exhales of his foul cigarettes, he had exposed most of mankind while working for his Rimini paper. Political corruption, business corruption, institutional corruption—all of it had been his beat in the Adriatic resort. And then there were the Germans who descended on Rimini's beaches every summer for their tans—he had plenty of stories about "those Nazis" too, so many of them that he had been better off taking early retirement and seeing Rome from Flavio's *pensione*. He wouldn't go so far as to say there was a contract out on him, but why be sorry when he could be safe? What did he mean exactly? The Germans were after him? He shrugged and blew more smoke. For him to know and me to find out. The closest to a fact I gleaned from him was when I told him about Glasses taking notes on Tonio's activities, and he shrugged that off as the "usual jockeying" between the Interior Ministry National Police and the Defense Ministry *carabinieri*. "They always keep an eye on one another," Gianni said. "As long as they can keep proving corruption against one another, they have room to maneuver."

When Gianni himself ran out of maneuvering room, it had nothing to do with contract killers sent by the Nazis or anybody else. One morning I was roused from sleep by the new tenants, there as they were every day for fixing up the place before moving in. On this particular morning, they had found Gianni dead on his cubicle cot. Had I heard anything? Had he looked ill the night before? I answered those same questions several times more for the cops who started filling up the apartment in the uniforms of the Interior Ministry, Defense Ministry, and any other ministry that had anything to do with corpses. After about an hour, Flavio also showed up, summoned by the new tenants with suspicions that he had left them with somebody who should have been in a hospital a long time before. I didn't like the way they looked at me as another potential burden of the same kind.

After hours of questions and statements both in the apartment and at the Questura, I ended up at a café with Flavio. I didn't realize how shaken I was until my third coffee, although by then, it might have also been the coffee cavorting in my arm and leg muscles. The preliminary findings of the medical examiner were that Gianni had died of a heart attack sometime during the night—or, as I thought of it, a few hours after he had told me about the German movie star he had exposed as a pedophile and had added to his list of the people after him. Flavio, looking a lot less bedraggled than he had when running the *pensione*, scoffed at the idea.

"The man worked for his newspaper as a bookkeeper," he said, as though it were common knowledge. "He took retirement because his heart was bad." How did he know that? "All his stories were starting to impress Daniela, so I asked Tonio to look him up. She stopped being impressed."

So much for the hand-kissing. Then I reminded him he had left out the bookkeeper particular despite all the chances he'd had to provide it at the station, on the way back and forth from the station, at the Ambra Jovinelli, on the way back and forth from the Ambra Jovinelli, etcetera, etcetera. He agreed—in a way. There was a nod, maybe a *mea culpa* look, but most of all, another of those shamed expressions. "And if you knew he was making up everything, then what?" he asked. "He'd see it on your face. He'd already seen it on everybody else's. Let him have one place where he could tell his lies and believe in them. He had a right to his dreams, too, didn't he?"

I hoped my eyes didn't look icy.

ACROSS THE WIDE MISSOURI

I have always pictured loneliness as being in a strange city on a Sunday afternoon and walking across a bridge. It doesn't matter if the bridge is an imposing span such as the Golden Gate in San Francisco or a modest crossing over a European river or canal. Upon reflection, I suppose there is no great novelty to this. A bridge is a symbol of getting from Point A to Point B, but within strange surroundings the Point B is unlikely to be a fulfilling arrival, strongly belying a sense of orientation. And that water underfoot is too much of a reminder of an anonymous flow. Who knows how far the tide would take a body if I had an accident and how long before I was missed? The Sunday afternoon part? That is when closed shops emphasize the home, the personal, and the intimate happening then or later in the evening— everything to which the stranger is an outsider. As you might tell, I have spent a few ponderous moments on this question.

Granted that some of this mood attack might be alleviated by entering a bar or cafe for a drink. But I have never liked drinking by myself or, for that matter, when the sun is still keeping the tab. For their part, museums, zoos, and aquariums appeal the way a Salvation Army kitchen does to a hungry drifter: Bad enough to waft through institutions created for my problem, but to be identified ahead of time for it is doubly oppressive. So no Miros, snow leopards, or manta rays. And no also to napping through the ominous hour. Waking up again all cotton-mouthed has never cured anything. All of which has often left a movie house as the solution to afternoon angst. However bad the picture, there will always be another one in re-emerging into the street—the one where the city lights have taken effect, the restaurants have volunteered for the weekend's last free hours, and laughter clinks like ice cubes. *Then* is the hour for a bar or cafe, with better odds against having to drink to the bottom of the glass without company.

But first there is the movie, and the first time it was a solution was not in a foreign city; Brooklyn just felt like one. My parents and brother had gone off for the weekend to some Poconos cabin with an aunt and uncle, a trip I was able to get out of thanks to a school paper I was scheduled to deliver on Monday. Against calculations that the whole weekend would be needed for the task, I had everything ready to go by early Sunday morning. The day suddenly sprawled out before me seemed to call for something ambitious—both for exercise and as a reward for disposing of the school assignment so quickly. I didn't leave the house determined to cover the several miles to the Brooklyn Bridge, but one neighborhood downtown dissolved smoothly into the next, and that is where I ended up. I had such a sense of achievement in this marathon that what I eventually recognized as loneliness did not hit me until I reached the end of the bridge in Manhattan, deciding that I had gone far enough, that it was time to start back. But to what exactly? I had seen it all on the way down. Now there would just be a feeling of climbing back up the hill even if the terrain didn't actually pose that challenge. Why would anyone have boxed himself into the need to have to do something so stupid?

I made it back up to the Flatbush Avenue Extension with the growing thought that it was strange that I should be walking past so many people without knowing any of them. That might have been boilerplate sociology for urban planners, but it wasn't for me. And it also struck me that all these strangers weren't precisely strange in any dictionary meaning of the word. Except for a scruffy old-timer selling pencils who for some reason had shaved off half of his Hitler mustache, the men, women, and children circulating on all sides of me defined the bland, whether white, black, or Latino no suggestion of mystery in their faces. I didn't know any of them personally, but I had the sluggish feeling I didn't have to in order to know them. At the moment, they were out walking the streets, but soon they would be home doing household things, nothing at all startling in their daily routines. I had embarked on a marathon walk, so why couldn't they have done something, been something, or merely thought something out of the ordinary? Ambulatory as they might have been, they were as passive as the trains docked in the LIRR rail yard—waiting for an engineer eventually to get on for moving them where they would never go on their own and to just a fixed track anyway. Their whole lives shaped up as a series of restrictions.

Across the street from the rail yard was the Spanish-language Atlantic movie house. I had passed it often, sometimes stopping to take in the discolored stills of Pedro Armendariz, Dolores del Rio, and other Mexican actors I recalled from small parts in Hollywood productions. At the very least, I told myself, whatever the picture now playing was, it would have people in it more interesting than those I had been passing to and from the Brooklyn Bridge.

The cashier, a graying woman, used to dealing with Anglo riffraff, tried her best to talk me out of going in. "There are no subtitles," she kept saying. "Go to that place up the street."

The subtitles particular hadn't occurred to me until it was mentioned, but it was too late to back out. I could have told her I was a graduate student in Spanish, but it was easier smiling like Johnny Nice Guy as I nudged the five-dollar bill closer to her. She sighed.

The movie on the screen was almost as discolored as the stills around the box office. Since it was a normal Sunday afternoon for a lot of other people, there were several clusters of families—mother, father, kids—around the orchestra. The place smelled of cherries. I had the darkness of a night scene to thank for only two people giving me an extra look as I groped down for an aisle seat. One of them was curious but more interested in the picture, the other one indignant about having his attention to the screen interrupted. I would have told him to train his eyes ahead if I had known any of those words in Spanish.

It took about a minute to know I had made the right decision to come in. Not because of the movie exactly, whose title I hadn't seen or had seen but couldn't remember. Whatever its title, it was one scene after another of *caballeros* spitting at one another while I wondered how they managed to stay on their feet under sombreros that should have tipped them over on their faces. The only women in sight were two maternal types who despised each other more than their *caballero* sons did one another; ugliness was in the air, and no one was reaching for a guitar. But none of that mattered. What made sitting there good, even exciting, was that I had advanced beyond the familiar and had found company for it while still unsure what was coming next. For all I knew, some of the glistening studs might fall off the starched leggings of the *caballeros*, and I would be there to witness it!

Some years passed before I had reason to recall that Sunday afternoon in the Atlantic. I hadn't forgotten it; I just hadn't been in a situation similar enough to reawaken details so viscerally. Then I was. A bridge again—this time the Joan of Arc Bridge over the Seine in Rouen. Alone again—this time waiting for friends from Paris the next day. A Sunday again—although the French knew it as Dimanche. What I had counted on as a big difference from the Atlantic, however, was the language question. After years of *The Song of Roland* in school, what could deter me from entering the Gaumont cinema and following every word? Certainly not a lack of subtitles as back at the Atlantic. I had no trouble with the title of *Traitement de Choc*, did I? And stars Alain Delon and Annie Girardot I had seen any number of times. What could go wrong?

The Song of Roland, it turned out. It took a few exchanges to work out, but the characters in *Traitement de Choc* didn't recite eleventh-century epic poems to one another, least of all the stanza or two I had memorized. Instead, they were obsessed with casual street conversation, heaping all kinds of nouns, verbs, and other things in between *Bonjour* and *a bientot.* Embarrassment reigned over the orchestra. People were living and dying up on the huge screen, but I was already buried in my seat. That very morning I had read a local paper without a problem between one cathedral and another, had even swum through a marsh of French politics without drowning, but in the darkness of *Traitement de Choc*, I wasn't even able to resort to my cafe *celui, cella.* Neither Delon nor Girardot was able to see my pointing finger. It was a Shock Treatment, all right.

I told myself to get a grip, and it seemed to work: Delon uttered two whole sentences with words I understood. Or was that because he had made so many American movies that his French wasn't what it could have been anymore? Never mind. At worst, we were in it together. The trouble was Girardot and her half-swallowed, rapid-fire delivery. Worse, she played a character endangered for her curiosity about the secret to the so-called miracle rejuvenation treatment offered to women in a luxurious spa. This made for a lot of mutterings to herself and for leading questions to suspects that should have made the audience ride along with her suspicions. The flaw there was that if you didn't understand the leading question, it led nowhere.

I hadn't been reduced to complete witlessness. I knew before Girardot that the secret to the anti-aging spa treatment was breeding the cells cut from the Portuguese studs ostensibly hired as waiters with the perks of bedding down the guests. It wasn't too much of a mystery, either, that the villain piling up the corpses of what was left of the Portuguese was the head doctor Delon. I really wanted to warn Girardot not to fall in lust with him, but she didn't seem able to read my thoughts in English. And that ended up too bad for all of us—when Girardot discovered Delon's specialization and stabbed him to death, when the police didn't believe her story about the cell breeding and arrested her for murder, and when I naively waited for her exoneration scene that never came. Instead, there was only FIN. That word I understood.

FIN wasn't exactly what you would call a subtitle, but I had to give the French credit for trying. On another afternoon in Copenhagen, that was the least of my problems. I'm sure the cinema had a name, but what it had more importantly during a downpour was an old-fashioned marquee that extended out to the curb. Nothing says disconsolate more effectively than trudging through the rain in wet shoes, and nothing offers an inviting harbor more opportunely than a marquee announcing *Die Engel von St. Pauli*. The stills promised sultry women in or out of bras or something in between and guns, lots of guns. Whoever the Angel of St. Pauli was, he didn't seem to spend a lot of time on the head of a pin.

The first revelation was that the picture was in German but with subtitles in English rather than Danish. That seemed to imply either that the producers didn't want to spend caption money for one small language group or assumed that Danes deserved their reputation as linguistically flexible. A second revelation was that hyper sound volume made everyone shout like the Gestapo knocking on a door. And nobody was more suited for such a role than leading man Horst Frank, a Klaus Kinski on his meds in a shining black raincoat that seemed to have been strapped on him. His most trustworthy look was the chill of an interrogator.

With the help of the subtitles, it should have been easy to figure out whether Frank was the angel of the title while he rolled around Hamburg's red-light district with the hookers and motorbike gangs. The problem there was that the projectionist didn't want to give away too many secrets gratis, so had jumbled the order of the reels he shot through his little window. Every 15 or 20 minutes, a yellow celluloid strip interrupted screen events, followed by a different location with hoods or cops agreeing to meetings with other characters who had died in some previously projected reel. Not counting a growl here and there and one guy who marched indignantly back toward the box office, this brought out the fabled good humor of the Danes, some of whom began to shout across the orchestra in competition in imagining who would be the next Lazarus. Horst Frank disappointed a pair in front of me by playing through coherently for two reels, but then he won them back by visiting an old hooker friend dying in the hospital who had already died. Once a long time ago, I remembered, I had criticized people in Brooklyn for leading overly regulated lives. But what had been more regulated than my assumption that some Grade Z cops-and-robbers trash from Germany proceeded from A to B to C? Lucky for me, the Danes woke me up to knowing better.

After a few years there, I had no problems with language in Rome. With a family and many friends, I couldn't complain, either, about drifting around the city alone and dwelling on what far shore the Tiber might drop me after taking a header. That's probably why it seemed like a kind of challenge to old demons when I went for a walk one Sunday afternoon by myself. The bridge part came easily in crossing the Ponte Garibaldi into Trastevere, into a good quarter- mile of movie houses scattered around every few blocks on and off the main Viale Trastevere. The cheapest of the houses belonged to a Vatican-owned network that might not have brought in as much as tourists to the Sistine Chapel did, but they added up to bigger numbers than those at Sunday Mass. If there was such a thing as third-run houses for content, the Vatican places answered the call in an assortment of sex comedies, Horst Frank-like dramas, and the occasional Italian classic broken free from rights issues. There were also ancient Hollywood films with long-gone actors. One of these playing that afternoon at the Esperia was *Across the Wide Missouri* with the very late Clark Gable as an 1800s trapper bent on marrying a Blackfoot teenager no matter the cost in frontier frictions. What better movie to see in the heart of old Rome?

Inside was a small square box of a space that had the odor of a recently evacuated junk shop. Seven or eight rows of hard chairs requisitioned from a cell block had been screwed into the floor before a spottled screen that might have appealed to collectors of abstract art. There were only three people in the place—two Italian soldiers who greeted my arrival with a duet of braying yawns and an old woman in a shawl fast asleep. No reason not to think that Vatican agents had found their print of *Across the Wide Missouri* in the rubble of a collapsed building and had seen an opportunity for adding to their poor box.

The so-called lights went from bleary to black as MGM's lion roared on the screen. It was the last English I heard for an hour and a half. Little surprise on that score since Italy had made a practice of dubbing films since a paranoid Mussolini had feared anti-Fascist foreign powers slipping propaganda into on-screen dialogue and since postwar producers had realized that dubbing was cheaper than live sound. But what I hadn't known was that Italy didn't *completely* dub foreign imports and that *Across the Wide Missouri* was one of the exceptions. In his striving for greater authenticity, director William Wellman had insisted on his Blackfoot characters speaking the Rockies Chinook jargon they used with white fur traders. Apparently lacking an Italian-Chinook dictionary, the Italians had preserved those parts of the original soundtrack so that half the movie was in Italian and the other half in Chinook.

The soldiers weren't happy about it.

"Ma che cazzo! Cosa stanno dicendo?"

"Parlano indiano."

"Indiano! Ma che cazzo! Siamo noi indiani?"

No, none of us were Indian. Who could argue with them? But everything was so out of whack it was hard recalling when it had been *in* whack. Gable opening his mouth and sounding like Roberto Benigni being smothered. Ricardo Montalban—Mr. Fantasy Island, the bullshit ads pushing Corinthian leather, the wrathful Khan—as the villainous Blackfoot. And next to him, J. Carroll Naish, the Irish-born nobleman who had gained fame with *Life with Luigi*, navigating his Canuck dialogue without a single "how" or "forked tongue." The soldiers didn't know half of what they didn't understand.

And neither did I. It was sometime later that I discovered that what I had seen as *Across the Wide Missouri* was actually about half of what Wellman had shot, that MGM bigwigs had been furious with all the Chinook talk and simply so confused by the turns Gable's fur trapper had taken toward the Blackfoot characters—wanting to be friends, wanting to exploit them, wanting to marry them, having a child with his bride, losing his bride to wicked Montalban, killing Montalban, whisking away his child before it became too influenced by Blackfoot ways, returning the child to the tribe, etc.—that they decided American audiences wouldn't follow the story better than the Italian soldiers, so they took an ax to it and hired a narrator to patch over what was essentially unpatchable. Afterthoughts were usually like that, like trying to make sense of why Horst Frank was plotting to kill the dead and why the cells of studs from Portugal were more effective for rejuvenating bourgeois French women than those pulled out of Polish priests. In for a sprocket, in for a reel.

The Esperia's light bulb came back up just in time to see that the old lady asleep in her aisle seat was tipping over and about to fall to the ground. I got to her at the same time as one of the soldiers. She was so adamant about not opening her eyes I thought she was dead. But then she belched loud enough to scare fur trappers out of the Rockies. And there was no mistaking the smell running out with the belch. *"E ubriaca!"* the soldier said in disgust to make it official.

A drunken old lady was the final insult for him after all the Chinook talk. Without waiting for his friend to catch up, he marched up the aisle toward the exit, slapping every lowered seat back along the way. Not even the loud clacking stirred the old lady. Clearly, she was in no rush to go back to the evening streets and cross more bridges.

THE SEASONS OF OUR LOVE

Clint Eastwood's most unheralded film was undoubtedly *Hereafter*. With a perspective mostly associated with a history channel, it told three parallel stories of encounters with death without recourse to the Tales from the Crypt genre. One story dealt with a psychic's misgivings, a second with twins ripped apart by a fatal accident, the third with a French TV journalist who barely survives the 2004 Indian Ocean tsunami while on vacation with her lover-boss. In more than one detail, *Hereafter* indicates that while in Italy making westerns with Sergio Leone decades earlier, Eastwood didn't spend free time slouching at a sidewalk cafe listening to the fountains. Instead, he absorbed a sensibility that had very little to do with Dirty Harry.

This emerged most vividly in the story of the journalist played by Belgian actress Cecile de France (in itself a casting far afield from even *Unforgiven* and *Million Dollar Baby).* In shock since being brought back from drowning, laboring to accept that she has actually confronted death, she returns to Paris sure only that she cannot go on as she has been, that her near-death experience demands more from the rest of her life. Two sequences point up Eastwood's long-dormant European touch. The more subtle is an overtly simple tracking shot of the journalist and her lover going to their table in an upscale restaurant. Being media notables, they own their surroundings but not quite. Unlike the stunning entering of the Copacabana in Martin Scorsese's *Good Fellas*, the scene eschews dazzling technique for an inbred elegance that makes clear that the pair are not complete strangers to being treated well but as apt to be eating out of a can in their kitchens the following evening. In a sense, they are still on vacation, leaning on reserves of natural style in defining themselves for the occasion. There is nothing American, let alone Hollywood, about the flow to their table, more like an instinctive waft that the director is able to project from inside.

The second scene takes place in a TV station conference room where the journalist and her colleagues are discussing a projected program about the career of late President Francois Mitterand. And discuss it they do, arguing in detail about this and that policy of the chief-of-state. While other directors might have cut away after a minute or two for simultaneous action in another office or jumped-cut to something else after the meeting, Eastwood presses on with the scene, confident that his audience is familiar enough with Mitterand and can judge the emotional state of de France's character through her arguments, academic, glib, or penetrating, whatever they may be. Eastwood assumed an intelligent, well-read audience—one as interested in tricky economic maneuvers by a recent French leader as interested in cops manipulating robbers and robbers manipulating the cops. The character's intellect counted as much as her feelings and coming at a junction of personal crisis. The more she goes into Mitterand, and there had to be a lot of that *more*, the more she obviously has something else on her mind.

The first time I came across this kind of confidence so blatantly in a commercial film was in Italy's *Le Stagioni del Nostro Amore* (*The Seasons of Our Love*). *Seasons* came along in the wake of Italy's own tsunami (of a cinematic type) in the 1960s when the operatic narrative of Luchino Visconti's *Rocco snd His Brothers*, the extravagant carnival of Federico Fellini's *La Dolce Vita*, and the austerity of Michelangelo Antonioni's *L'Avventura* arrived in America within days of each other. The wildly diverse pictures confirmed Italy as the most fertile film-making country well through the decade, with players such as Marcello Mastroianni, Gabriele Ferzetti, Anouk Aimee, and Monica Vitti becoming as known beyond the continent as they had been on it for a few years. It didn't hurt that the leading players were all glamorous in one way or another.

But they were also something else, as were most of the films in which they appeared. If there was a unifying quality to what were otherwise different visions by Visconti, Fellini, and Antonioni, as well as to the personalities of their leading characters, it was languor. Whatever social standing they had, Visconti's immigrant boxers in Milan, the flippant Via Veneto glitterati of Fellini, and Antonioni's idling upper middle classes were all citizens of the postwar nation that might have gotten rid of Mussolini but had become citizens of the alleged Italian Miracle in which social progress and political corruption were indistinguishable and within which combative energy was at a premium. Governments rose and fell, but often for no better reason than the Minister of This envisioned a greater profit in becoming the Minister of That. The ruling Christian Democrat party had the backing of the Vatican and the United States but wouldn't have fared all that well on an examination about either Christianity or democracy. Opposition Communists kept their distance from Moscow but for critics, Resistance songs and enthusiastic rank-and-files notwithstanding, with a little too much passive-aggressiveness (or maybe aggressive passivity) toward the Christian Democrats. And between them, not so much in the middle as in recesses of one or the other, was a constellation of Socialist parties brandishing their leftism or their moderation as the occasion invited.

Against this background ideology and a dedication to it were not automatically renewed subscriptions. If it wasn't Leonard Cohen's "Everybody Knows," it was at least Peggy Lee's "Is That All There Is?" This was the landscape director Florestino Vancini sought to illuminate with *The Seasons of Our Love*. If he ultimately failed at the effort, it wasn't due to personal languors in putting the production together since he had to talk everyone involved in it to work for scale after big producers such as Dino De Laurentiis backed away from its political content. Ironically, said political content was in its own way a paean to the De Laurentiis world, X-raying why it had little to fear from the nation's traditional Left. But that paranoia was also an ingredient of the era's social ennui. It wasn't until two years after its release that *Seasons* acquired a striking relevance, and not merely for the lengthy celluloid discussion of the *Hereafter* kind.

The framework for *Seasons* was the road movie, through the northern region of Lombardy in the company of 40-year-old Vittorio (Enrico Maria Salerno), a journalist in crisis. We know that he is in crisis because he tells us he is, and not just once. He has left a wife, daughter, and lover behind and is bent on returning to his birthplace in Mantua in the frail hope that it will scatter the ghosts that have been haunting him into an increasingly torpid state. There are problems with Vittorio. One is that, as dramatized by his relations with his wife, daughter, and lover, he is a cold fish—an isolating presence only accentuated by his long stretches behind the wheel. Because of Salerno's extremely centered performance, stop-offs for a coffee can be as much of a relief for the viewer as for him.

A second problem is in the details of the memories (revealed in flashbacks) he indulges as he drives along. Although they cover the recognizable highs and lows of a midcentury Italian, including his actions as a Resistance fighter, they are pretty prosaic, failing to lend urgency to Whatever Happened to Vittorio and Why Is He So Glum? Suggesting that Vancini himself didn't know, he has Vittorio's old flame Francesca (Anouk Aimee) ask precisely that, and all she gets for her trouble is a big sulk. Worse, she asks him in the middle of disillusioning him of any notion that he can retrieve her from his past. And yet worse than that? She confesses that when he had proposed marriage to her years ago, "I almost laughed in your face." This acid about his youthful impracticality doesn't go down any more easily coming from an attractive woman comfortable in her own married life and with her assumption that others can talk about life's bumps and bruises as philosophically as she can. On the contrary, that only widens the chasm between the now-middle-aged pair.

If the encounter with Francesca straightens out more twists than he had welcomed, Vittorio's visit to his Resistance comrade Leonardo (Gian Maria Volonte) threatens to tie him within himself interminably. Triggering a debate between the men is the Brezhnev Doctrine, the Kremlin's justification for interfering in the affairs of any Warsaw Pact country accused of jeopardizing the solidity of the Eastern European bloc. Like other old comrades Vittorio has already visited for restoring his faith in Communist principles, Leonardo is more fellow penitent than confessor, apologizing for a whole series of domestic priorities that have diluted a political commitment. And anyway, they had never fought for the Brezhnev Doctrine, had they? As in his earlier reunions, Vittorio struggles for a cogent reply.

When I saw *The Seasons of Our Love*, my knowledge of the Brezhnev Doctrine was that Leonid Brezhnev was the secretary of the Soviet Communist Party, that he had an unpleasant scowl, and that any doctrine attributed to him probably didn't endorse greater pursuits of happiness. That two characters in a prominent motion picture could be debating the pros and cons of his fiat seemed to be an expropriation from a scholastic journal or Communist cell meeting. The scene was intriguing, novel, even daring, having no Hollywood parallel with, say, Paul Newman and Steve McQueen arguing about the Gulf of Tonkin resolution. It wasn't torn from the headlines, as they say, but from an OpEd page and with the evident expectation that orchestras and balconies would not stir restlessly.

Less than two years later, the Brezhnev Doctrine lost any sniff of the academic, becoming the subject of every media outlet in the world with the invasion of Czechoslovakia by the Soviet Union, East Germany, Poland, Hungary, and Bulgaria. For many Italian communists, the invasion was the breaking point in spite of the fact that their party had been among the first to condemn it. But the Vittorios and Leonardos in the Vancini film had not really needed the invasion to rationalize their languor; if anything, it was a *deus ex machina* for their consciences.

Seasons also foreshadowed something else. The film's climactic sequence finds Vittorio at a beachfront bar overrun by young people frolicking around a jukebox. This drives him into a self-pitying fury, throwing around every object he touches. He has reached the winter of his love, (symbolically) been surpassed by a new generation that owes nothing to his paralysis. That will introduce new hills and valleys in Italy over the next few decades, but it will not be Vittorio's topography. Birthplace included, he has become a stranger in his own land.

There is a markedly paradoxical line from Vancini's *Seasons* to Eastwood's *Hereafter.* On the one hand, the Italian film fades out as bleakly as possible, a mood not too different from how Eastwood ended his masterpieces *Unforgiven* and *Million Dollar Baby.* But if a European sensibility, especially that of the 1960s, circulated here and there in *Hereafter,* it did not surrender to the ideological gloom of the period. In fact, it could even be scored for ultimately falling back on Hollywood's addiction to happy endings in the attempt at bringing the three parallel stories together before the final fadeout. To wit, the French journalist, while still uncertain of what she saw as she was drowning, writes a best-selling book about it; she gives an autographed copy to the psychic whose powers are revived by touching her autograph so that he can reassure her that she did indeed encounter death; and the psychic trembles with another message that the dead twin has not lost sight of his despondent, surviving brother. If you don't believe in psychics, the ending is ludicrous. If you believe in old-time Hollywood practices, it's par for the course. If you believe in zombie-less and vampire-less death as the intellectual premise for a commercial picture, you will have to be open to more than one sensibility.

THE SWARM

Rare is the list of the all-time worst movies that doesn't include Ed Wood's *Plan 9 from Outer Space.* Or some of those creature features of the 1950s when atomic testing was blamed for magnifying everything from spiders to housewives and setting them amok on cardboard cities. Or maybe one of those cop tales that take place exclusively in a police office consisting of a desk, a water cooler, and tough talk. But bad as these pictures could be, they had a common element of cheesiness— if they hadn't been shot in less than a week, it was only because a fire had melted the camera. With expectations low from the start, being an all-time worst was not nearly as much of a consideration as being able to plug product—and *product* in the most generic sense it was—into a rural drive-in or city itch house. The evaluations of camp, satire, and subtle commentary on the theory of relativity came from film schools later.

The real Worst, though, has to be sought elsewhere. A minimal requirement is waste—in the money spent, in the neurons squandered, in the artistic reputations trashed. The Big has to open the curtain for the Least, with stereophonic sound, Cinerama vistas, and 3-D interactions encouraged if not required. A second necessity is pretentiousness—no matter how banal the action on the screen, it has to be a dire warning to civilization. Thirdly, the technological advances enlisted for the picture must not disguise the crudest table-top stop-motion practices; i.e., rear screen projection has to look like actors riding carousel horses in a studio sound stage, cave-ins have to look like Raisin Bran toppling down into breakfast bowls, blastoffs to Mars have to look very much like fountain pens escaping from shirt pockets. The less adroit these illusions, the more qualified for the Worst.

Candidates from recent decades alone abound, and that's not counting *How the West Was Won*, which escapes the Worst category thanks to an episode of covered wagons with annoying actors being swept into providentially churning rapids. A western deserving more meditation is *Mackenna's Gold*, which meets the star-power burden with Gregory Peck, Omar Sharif, Edward G. Robinson, Lee J. Cobb, Eli Wallach, and just about every other major character actor from the last century. Its depiction of a mountain collapse resembles that of a layer cake splattering the counter at your favorite bakery, the accompanying rumbling the after-lunch indigestion of its producers, while the endless double-crossing narrative became so boring that the director got rid of half the cast of luminaries in a montage about five seconds long. As more than one critic couldn't refrain from observing at the picture's opening, *Mackenna's Gold* redefined pyrite.

Other finalists in the Premium Worst category would be every other disaster movie, especially with Shelley Winters as a pain in the ass of a Jewish Mother Earth, but they get eliminated for that single scene of the tsunami, meteor, or magma making its initial impact, justifying the special effects budget and allowing some swiftly dead character to exclaim "Oh, my god!" Coming close to an exception is *Earthquake*, where even the cardboard came from the basement of Home Depot, and scenes of destruction resembled the morning after in a frat house. But *Earthquake* avoids Worst designation by having only a very tired-looking Ava Gardner and Charlton Heston's jaw as stars in the classic sense as we wait for the otherwise B cast to get clocked by a beam, building, or some other object that was cheaper than a screenwriter.

Conversely, there is the specimen of *The Chase*, which not only has a platinum cast (Marlon Brando, Robert Redford, Jane Fonda, Robert Duvall, etc.) but was directed by Arthur Penn and written by Lillian Hellman. Given all these precious metals, the film's escaped convict premise atop its dire warning to civilization atop a sadistic fervor for beating up all its leading characters atop another dire warning to civilization should have put it among the favorites for Worst, but it had so many Greek choruses (Janice Rule and Henry Hull most conspicuously) that it came off as one big wink, not really caring if civilization was warned as long as nobody's check bounced. If pretentiousness were the sole mark of a Premium Worst picture, *The Chase* would be hard to beat, but the category has more rigorous standards.

And the winner? It is hard to find a more enervating entry than The Swarm when all the scores are toted up. Among its other attributes, I thought it was going to kill me. For real.

As betrayed by its title, *The Swarm* is about bees—a lot of bees (800,000, according to the producers) of a killer African variety. To deal with this threat, *The Swarm* rounded up an Oscar-heavy cast of Michael Caine, Henry Fonda, Jose Ferrer, Olivia de Havilland, Patty Duke, Lee Grant, and Ben Johnson, throwing in Richard Widmark, Richard Chamberlain, Katherine Ross, and Fred MacMurray for modesty. All starts ominously enough when the bugs overrun a U.S. military base. It gets worse for characters on the screen and the orchestra when this prompts a two-hour debate between scientist Caine who urges a scientific solution, and military area commander Widmark who is ready to blow up the planet to avoid getting stung.

I was on Caine's side even though his adenoidal calm was a little less engaged in the problem than Widmark's contempt for anyone not in uniform. I was also annoyed with my doctor, who hid behind a programmatic "we'll do some tests" when he didn't like what my heart had told his stethoscope. As Widmark could have reminded him, science wasn't everything. But off I went to see heart specialists, as off the preteen Paul in *The Swarm*, bored with the ants crawling over a family picnic blanket. went off for a closer inspection of a bunch of bees buzzing in a nearby tree. A moment or two later, Paul was an orphan and had lots of ugly marks on his body. News of the attack was all that Caine needed to warn Widmark (and civilization) that they were up against an exceptional antagonist. Widmark did not reply with one of his sadistic Tommy Udo giggles from *Kiss of Death*, but he seemed tempted.

The crux of the heart examinations were stress tests, which began with sitting around in a waiting room transported from the Port Authority bus terminal, shopping bags, knapsacks, and iPads included. Not only was eating permitted, it was dictated for patients to judge changes in the system before and after scans. The old-timer sitting next to me would be judged based on an onion sandwich. "Most jerks use onions just to cover up other crap," he clucked. "That's spoiling the onions. Got to eat them straight. And they do a good job screwing with those machines inside, too."

"How do you know that?"

"I'm here for the fourth time. Haven't found a damn thing in the ticker yet. That's the onions."

"Good to know."

"Worse that can happen, onions are as much bullshit as pills. Lose-lose all around. I can wait."

What the little town in *The Swarm* was waiting for was a black sky of killer bees. This was bad news insofar as the imminent invasion corresponded to a founders day celebration in which the de Havillands, Johnsons, and MacMurrays got to deliver their one line of dialogue for earning their name on the film posters. It was good news in that this let the story funnel all these big-named extras into the same train destined for disaster and not have to go on too long with a romantic subplot. Of three 70-year-olds dancing around each other since de Havilland had been Melanie in *Gone With the Wind*, Johnson had started galloping through hills, rivers, and prairies for John Ford, and MacMurray had claimed whatever ineffectual character was available. Instead of going through a few more decades to decide who was in love with whom, at least they were going to die together.

The train pulled out of town with the swarm in overhead pursuit. The passengers got excited, then got the 800,000 bees on them and got more excited. In the locomotive, the engineer shooed at them until he went off the track and into a gulley. The bad news was that everyone was killed. The good news was that there was only a second or two to discern the trestle table from which the toy train had toppled. Best of all news was that the camera stayed far enough away from the scene not to make out the dummies laying around the gulley.

The train massacre gave even Widmark pause, time enough to have Caine invite in his old mentor, the wheelchair-bound Fonda, to find the vaccine that would save civilization. While Fonda took up residence in a lab the size of a broom closet, Chamberlain ran over to check that a nuclear power plant (it was a crowded neighborhood) under Ferrer's administration remained impregnable to the bees. He arrived just in time to listen to Ferrer's bluster about how they were all safe, then went down the silo with everybody else when the bees decided the plant was the ultimate honey stick. There was a lot of screaming from the plant employees as they went thrashing around, but on the positive side, Ferrer shut up.

The stress began before the stress test. The doctor and two assistants were disappointed to learn that I had broken a hip in a softball game some years before and had lost almost an inch off that leg in surgery. Disappointment followed disappointment when they discovered that the raised heel on my loafer was the only one I had, no special Nikes in my closet. Didn't I know that I couldn't jog on their treadmill in loafers? No, I didn't . . . All right, all right, We'll just have to use a pill. A pill? Like an onion? What are you talking about? Just get on the table, and we'll give you the pill. Get him some water!

Fonda grew impatient with his dry runs. He was sure he had a candidate for the right vaccine, but he needed to test it on humans, not just rodents. Caine told him not to do something stupid, Fonda assured him he wouldn't, then Caine did something stupid of his own by leaving Fonda alone with a hypodermic and machines that went beep beep beep. Fonda gave himself a vaccine injection, then began sweating as the machines registered his blood pressure to unprecedented heights. But just as he was about to collapse from the strain, the beeps began to go down again. He stopped sweating. He sat more erect in his wheelchair. He told his recorder that he had found an antidote to the bee stings. Fake-out, fake-out. No sooner had he said it than the beep-beep-beeps returned with even more astronomical blood pressure numbers. Fonda was still sweating when he joined the rest of the corpses.

The pill didn't taste like an onion, and the water tasted like water. What I was to keep in mind, the doctor declared, was that the pill would initially increase pressure in my chest, not perilous but for some people disquieting. I told her in advance that I promised to be disquieted. She thought that amusing, then wheeled around to watch the machines that had been wired to me. I didn't like the idea that her assistants hovered nearby in case they were needed, but I hadn't liked any idea ever since that damn softball game.

She hadn't been kidding: Bare seconds after swallowing the pill, my chest started quaking—a little squeeze at first, then something in the pincer vein. The doctor kept her eyes on the monitor, finding the zooming numbers reassuring for some perverted reason. One assistant nodded to second her reaction. The other looked like he just wanted to get out for a smoke. The more I tried to slow down my breathing, the more rapidly it came, and I didn't have to guess what the dew on my arms was about. There had to be an on the other hand, right? I mean, aside from not just seeing any bees on the ceiling, right?

I might have imagined worry in the eyes of the assistant antsy for his smoke, but that could have been anything—had he forgotten his Bic lighter, that was one possibility. What I didn't need to imagine was the other assistant moving away from the doctor to come over to me to pat me on the shoulder the way TV cops pat a bleeding victim to reassure him an ambulance is speeding to the scene. I didn't need thinking those victims usually died, and the TV cops looked sad for all of ten seconds afterward before moving on to livelier matters. I didn't need to, but I did anyway.

But I didn't die—not right away. The numbers did indeed start coming down as the chest pressure eased. I was so relieved that I glanced over to the monitor to see for myself how steadily the numbers were descending. Like all numbers showing on beep-beep-beep hospital machines, they were porous, too vulnerable to a nudge to reverse direction and start to rise again. I really couldn't figure out why my eyes had wanted to look at them.

"Pretty good," the doctor said.

There was a trace of admiration in her voice, but there would have been if she had been with Fonda after the opening round, too. Who could trust her reaction? Widmark was right about scientists.

And he didn't want any more of Fonda's experiments with the bees closing in on Houston, so he tried one last maneuver before he had to nuke the city: Burn it down. Fires were set everywhere with the theory that they would turn the bees to potato chips. But over a funk at Fonda's death, Caine went back to first principles: why had the bees attacked that military base in the first place? That was how it had all started, wasn't it?

If you believed in scientists like Caine, the answer was simple to the point of ludicrousness: the military base had been equipped to send out an alarm system that echoed far too perfectly the vibrations of a queen bee calling all to dinner, work, and other delights. *Noise*, in other words, had been the key all along, and it was only for the human species to create a similar noise and lead the bees Pied Piper style away from Texas to save civilization. The discovery couldn't have come at a better time for Widmark, whose fires had not only not stopped the bees but whose own skyscraper command post was under siege. When they even rode the elevators up to his floor, he had no choice but to resort to a flame thrower to give Caine time enough to get away to try out his noise theory. Widmark did not manage to burn many bees, but he succeeded in burning himself to death.

There was a feeling of an imminent end. *The Swarm* had run out of most of its actors, and I had run out of seconds between Wave One and Wave Two. The doctor instructed me to relax as if ordering the dying to stay alive was therapeutic. In her eyes, I couldn't be more obtuse than the swarms following after Caine's helicopters with the special queen sounds. Get me out over the sea, and I was also likely to be surprised by a second fleet of helicopters armed with a special oil concoction that, poured over the suddenly docile swarms, turned into the crisps Widmark had intended. In the end, therefore, it was a triumph for cooperation between science and the military.

Walking home from the specialists that day, I wanted to be happy for both sides. But deep down, where everything had turned out to be beating normally, I knew none of us had come through a moment we wanted to relive. Even on TV.

KNOWING THE KILLER

I always know who the killer is. I don't consider this either a gift or a curse, though some people have sought to persuade me it is one or the other. According to them, always knowing the killer implies extraordinary insight into human behavior or means I can't take pleasure from detective stories, national scandals, or international conspiracies. The two sides agree that (in the political cant of the day) it can't be easy for me to realize I'd known then what I know now.

Both the flattery and the pity are misplaced. Always being able to identify the killer is just intuition vindicated by suspect imaginations, and in this, I am hardly alone. Political rabble-rousers and media moguls, to name two groups, have displayed the same abilities to their immense social and financial gain. The only difference between us is the odd million people or odd billion dollars.

Okay, maybe one other difference, too. While the rabble-rousers and media moguls are always delighted to have their intuitions borne out, I rarely am. Forget how exasperating it might be not to be able to guess along with a detective hero until the near-end; actually, zeroing in on the killer with his first appearance on the page or screen can set in motion other chains of pleasures, foremost the one about seeing whether the creator in question *earns* his climactic unveiling. Similarly, I might grasp at once who is wearing the black hat in some sordid tabloid tale involving a public figure, but that doesn't necessarily prevent me from savoring over weeks and months the fine spirals of descent from denials and no-comments to admissions, apologies, and arrests.

In short, I've never confused myself with Orson Welles, about whom it was said he never truly enjoyed a movie because he was too practiced in all its separate artistic and technical ingredients. Whether true or not about Welles (and I doubt it is), it isn't my own brilliance that bothers me about my prompt identification of killers. As I see it, the real problem lies in the sheer predictability of so much of what passes these days for a mystery, fictional and non-fictional. It simply depresses me that others can regard "The Emperor's New Clothes" as a whodunit. We really have to work at so much naivete, and it says nothing good about us.

Start with fiction. As any bookstore browser or movie-goer can attest, we have traveled quite a distance from the once-standard plausibilities of homicidal envies, jealousies, and angers. The terrain around us today is more commonly dotted with lazy speculations about serial psychopaths, computer-generated thugs, or genocide-bent extraterrestrials. Even the extremes of human motivation have been shunted aside as being too bland, replaced by a science-fiction spirit of fixing ultimate blame on one kind of warped gene or another.

The convenient part of this trend for its creators is that they don't have to be any more responsible for their choices than their characters do. They can be as acrobatic—and insubstantial—as a *Matrix* entity. Even the logic that was stretched to the limits of elasticity with a yarn such as Agatha Christie's *Murder on the Orient Express* has lost whatever remained of its resilience with lack of inventive commitment to coherent plot and character: Instead of Everybody being revealed as the culprit, contemporary stories ricochet back and forth in structureless paranoia until, finally, Anybody steps out from behind the curtain. And on the off-chance that even Anybody might be construed as being too specific, insinuating a hard creative choice, there will be a few tacked-on endings—the first usually contradicting the thrust of the foregoing narrative, the second contradicting the first, and the third contradicting any residue of sense left. Within such an arbitrary, cynical perspective, how could I *not* know who the killer was?

The wiliest fiction minds are those that, aware of troublemakers like me, pretend to celebrate the classic forms of logical deduction so we'll stop our sniping. One of the best illustrations of this diversionary tactic was the long-running TV series *Columbo*. What, *Columbo* is not logical? Well, yes and no. The Peter Falk character himself was; he was nothing if not that. But while the internal mechanics of the hero's logic were usually impeccable, there was seldom sufficient credibility behind the manner in which he drafted the facts that activated his reasoning processes. The key to this hocus-pocus, and the popularity of the show for decades? We, the home viewers. We always knew precisely how each elaborate killing was carried out and for what motives. From this starting point, we then conceded knowledge, insights, and suspicions to the Falk hero that, objectively, couldn't be conceded most of the time. For crucial clues, in other words, the *Columbo* writers always depended on us to do their writing for them. We, in turn, were so presumptuous about what we knew that we forgot that the lieutenant, sly as he was, could not possibly have smelled something amiss about finding an ashtray on a left end-table instead of on the right one. We were given answers to questions that, as in some solipsistically demented version of *Jeopardy*, couldn't legitimately be asked of others. Or, as the *Columbo* creators might prefer it, we were accomplices before, during, and after the fact.

Columbo has hardly been alone among whodunits in relying on an audience for vital complicity; the motion picture and television industries have been obligated to that relationship for generations. More than once, Hollywood's investment in star image has meant compromising the logical conclusion of a given story. Perhaps the most notorious case occurred back in the big studio era when even Alfred Hitchcock feared making Cary Grant the murderer in *Suspicion*, bowing to front office pressures to re-edit the completed film so that it had a relatively happy ending and the star's fans ended up with a relatively familiar Cary Grant. Other performers have shied away from earning hisses with such career-first arguments as their desire to do only "positive characters" in suspense thrillers or their anxiety about doing two bad guys too close to one another. The point isn't that just our knowledge of these priorities through gossip columns, magazine shows, and the like thwarts guessing games in the orchestra ("So why couldn't they have stayed out of the picture altogether?"), but that we are seen as indispensable abettors of career tactics, however ruinously that function affects a given story's intelligibility.

Another kind of image factor is at work in the abasements known as reality shows. In the interests of remaining Topic A around the water cooler the following morning, program producers will see to it that the surviving apprentice, maggot-eater, or mate-swapper will be the creep or bitch who has made the most chilling case for life not being fair and for not wanting to make it any more so. This is called many things in the trade—staying ahead of the curve, pushing the envelope, taking a day off from worrying about role models—but what it comes down to is honoring the people you most want to see in Sumatra because then they won't be anywhere near your life. In fact, in this cathode sea of reality show sharks and their parasites, the only stations still upholding fabled honest grit as virtue are Nickelodeon, where reality is 20 years behind, the History Channel, where the program subjects all died on grainy newsreel film, and the Family Channel, in the hours before and after its transmission of the *700 Club*. As they say in sportscasting booths, again, a no-brainer.

My perceptiveness has been even less remarkable in arenas outside those traditionally associated with light entertainment. Indeed, when the killing has been very literally killing, I have yet to be compensated a single time for an ability mobs of others have turned to coin. Murder trial jurors, for instance, now go directly from the reading of a verdict to some interview where they identify themselves, their career desires, and the epiphanies that prompted their vote in the jury room. Crime scene technicians are still chalking the floors of Beverly Hills mansions when lawyers promote their firms by going on Fox to arraign and indict those taken into custody. Knowledge of the killer's identity has become such a presupposition for everyday affairs that pollsters spend as much time asking if we *care* who the villain is as soliciting views on his or her name. Whether it's a third cousin of Osama Bin Laden or American military jailers at Guantanamo, we are assumed to be so savvy as to have already progressed to having to choose among outrage, indifference, or some heartsick combination of the two in response to our discernment. Blank percent of us want the killer punished, blank percent of us want the culprit left alone because we've all been crumbs from that particular cookie at one time or another, and blank percent of us mainly want to be left alone. It is whodunit-by-plebiscite, a national game of Clue in which the pieces are maneuvered around the bored to gauge to what degree we actually are.

In recent years, Muslims have provided an important intersection in the identification of fictional and nonfictional killers. They have filled this role far more adequately than the previously invoked "Soviets," who never really included more than a handful of leering fat men in wide cardboard military epaulets or cheap brown suits weighed down with pawn shop medals. The Soviets were never the Russians, happy people who drink vodka and dance on table tops; they were just the Soviets, enemies not to be trusted near a nuclear bomb button.

The Muslims, on the other hand, are every swarthy who ever heard of the Koran. They are so ubiquitously the killer they can be deployed effectively as red herrings. Only after they have been grilled by all the top-rated investigators working for Dick Wolf Productions or left to rot in some immigration cell for a few years are they pronounced not guilty. They are Anybody as Everybody, and with such odds, it really doesn't matter if they did the particular crime in question or not since they are clearly capable of similar ones.

Some of this might sound as though knowing the killer's identity is simply a matter of recognizing what we have been told to see. So what? That's what Sherlock Holmes meant by elementary, wasn't it?

TWO BRANDOS

The classic bond between fathers and sons is usually said to be forged at the ballpark. The father talks about having seen Babe Ruth or Jackie Robinson or Tom Seaver, and the son rolls his eyes in pleas to be able to focus on those playing in front of him as the greatest of all time. History, even the baseball kind, is an abstraction for school Monday morning.

I forced my son Adam to roll his eyes more than once, abetted by an enthusiasm for the New York Mets that seldom offered him a plausible alternative on the field in front of him. Yes, the experience was supposed to be melding just for being in the stadium and eating hot dogs, but it really wouldn't have hurt if the local team had hit or caught the ball when it should have. Bringing a preteen to a ballpark to see a lousy team and filling in the blanks with great players from the Eisenhower years was like making him take a perp walk before he escaped to a more entertaining team, sport, or study of bees. Hot dogs were available at any supermarket.

Despite that forced labor, Adam became not just a baseball fan but at one point even worked for the Mets, both of us agreeing to forget a patch of rebellious years when the posters on his wall were attached to some other New York team. He remains the one and only member of my family actually to play on the field of the old Shea Stadium (a game among employees). But the ballpark wasn't the only place where we got to measure the commonalities, differences, and attritions between generations. Centuries before streaming, when even the multiplex was mainly hailed for being a smart advance in reducing society to so many cubicles, there was a structure known as the neighborhood movie house for accommodating fathers and sons. It was particularly hospitable on Saturdays when the feature was selected with an eye toward keeping younger viewers interested or sedated, whichever came first. This provided for a week of looking into other theaters in other neighborhoods rather than surrender to some intergalactic cartoon at hand around the corner. Father-son bonding could go just so far.

And then there was *Apocalypse Now*, the Vietnam War reverie directed by Francis Ford Coppola and loosely based on Joseph Conrad's *Heart of Darkness*. Some looses can be looser than others.

There were enough back stories for us with *Apocalypse Now* to furnish a library. One was basic for any parent: However responsible-thinking you might be, you do not insist that your 12 -year-old savor the pleasures of a picture about executive board room intrigues, terminal diseases, or both; he would have plenty of years ahead to indulge those delights for himself. There has to be the prospect of physical adventure, and if that means people shooting one another, the pieties can be put on hold until the trip home. Even then, it is better to focus on the implausibility of the hero firing twelves times from a six-shooter without having to reload. Every once in a while, realism can be useful.

That the shooting in *Apocalypse Now* occurred in Vietnam and Cambodia was an edgier problem since I had spent those years in anti-war activities, Adam knew it, and most characters dying in the picture were Special Forces types who might or might not have had it coming but who left big mournful holes in the screen in going down. There was a decided question as to whether the gunplay was received in the seat next to me in the same spirit as I had once seen Humphrey Bogart dismantle the Nazis. But that doubt turned out to be missing the jungle for the trees. By the time the bodies began to pile up, the movie had established its hallucinatory atmosphere of blaring rock, drug fantasies, volcanic explosions, colors defying the spectrum, and an overlaid narrative voice that would have been even creepier on my first viewing if I had known it was of Emilio Estevez doing the protagonist, his father, Martin Sheen. That the voiceover— not to mention much of the dialogue—was a ramble through a fog let me think of the picture's politics as a wash. Whatever

Apocalypse Now was for or against crossed over to the other side every time one of the crazed characters pulled a trigger, fixing it generically to one of its final dialogue lines—"the horror . . . the horror."

The speaker was a rogue Special Forces colonel portrayed by Marlon Brando as he expires. Brando's bald and grossly overweight Kurtz was more than one ocean away from the ex-pug Terry Malloy 25 years earlier in *On the Waterfront.* The actor had done slews of pictures in between, most notably his Oscar turn in *The Godfather,* but seeing Adam's absorption with Kurtz, I felt a small family circle being enclosed that contained more than screen performances. For more than one reason, *On the Waterfront* had been *the* movie when I had been his age. Gangsters and murders and betrayals and raising pigeons on cold rooftops—that had been only part of it. Count the particulars. Brando's exposed-nerves, propulsive presence as Malloy made other actors of the day register as Mrs. Brown's students doing a classroom recital of "O Captain! My Captain!" Whether or not we had ever seen, let alone been in, a boxing ring, there was no way we couldn't identify with Terry Malloy. He was a rebel still waiting to be told what to rebel against and not in too much of a hurry to figure out what it was since there were immediately surrounding comforts to be considered. He wasn't what he had once been as a contender before landing in Palookaville? Well, we weren't in kindergarten anymore, either. We shared his pain.

And he wasn't the only magnet in *On the Waterfront.* Anyone who had passed a Catholic girls school had come across Eva Marie Saint. On a bad day, we had also encountered a Karl Malden priest who behaved pugnaciously for the sake of behaving pugnaciously. Extras weren't extras; they were neighborhood people; they might not have been the longshoremen from *On the Waterfront*, but their calloused hands, weather-beaten faces, and yes, predictably cowed bluster wouldn't have been out of place unloading a freighter and forking over an extortion payment to the union if they wanted to work again the next day. And most of all, there was Lee J. Cobb's Johnny Friendly.

Every neighborhood had its Johnny Friendly, but not every family did. My family's was my uncle Ralph, who resembled Cobb enough with heavy jowls, deep bleating eyes, and glistening lips to be mistaken for the actor on the street. If that failed to cement the relationship, there was always my aunt's tart "Okay, Lee J!" when she was annoyed with him. Ralph didn't boss a corrupt waterfront union like Friendly, but he was equally attentive to the racing sheets and to a habit of squashing bills (mostly singles) into a shirt pocket if someone pleased him. That benevolence, however, shrank before what became known as his Money Game.

The Money Game was as much a part of holidays as Santa Claus was to Christmas and the Bunny Rabbit to Easter. The first ingredient of the Money Game was Ralph's addiction to standing and rattling a treasury of coins in his pants pockets. Maybe because of the cheap insurance policies he sold for a living, he never saw a bill that couldn't be broken down into quarters, dimes, and nickels and clumped into easy reach of his musical fingers. The second ingredient was a circle of nagging kids begging him all day to play the game—a chorus of charming innocence that, as the day wore on and Ralph pleaded for four or five more beers, reached lynch mob volume. Finally, with the other adults pleading with him to get it over with, he gathered all the kids in a bedroom to explain the rules. The most important was that anyone who threw a punch or gouged an eye would be sent out of the bedroom. As soon as that was on the record, he came out of his pockets with enough coins to feed every parking meter in Brooklyn.

Up all the coins went, over beds and dressers and nephews, and the scramble was on. The wrestling may not have had the same religious significance as young Greeks diving off Sheepshead Bay piers every year for an Orthodox cross, but the principle was the same—be the first to grab, and untold blessings would come your way. And through all the commotion, Uncle Johnny Friendly stood with a beatific smile, watching for fouls but mostly handicapping the winner to himself. It was a pose of uncontested power: What he saw was *his*. It was only later, after age had retired me from the Money Game, that the pose irked me twice over—once for itself and once for taking so long to be irked by it. Something was wrong with it and, as Malloy was given to grumbling in *On the Waterfront*, "that conscience thing" made the air a little thinner dwelling on it. Something—or somebody—was not what it was supposed to be. Deceit, sure. But maybe something beyond that? A betrayal? It had to be that. Betrayal always explained everything. Ask any teenager.

No context was riper for betrayal than *On the Waterfront.* Its central narrative of Terry Malloy waking up to testify against his corrupt father figure Johnny Friendly took place in the wake of the director Elia Kazan's willingness to name former leftist acquaintances as communists for the red-baiting House Un-American Activities Committee (HUAC). For many, Kazan was a rat collaborating in the blacklisting of numerous entertainment figures; for the filmmaker himself, the Malloy character was not a projection of what he had done away from the set on a national scale, just a tribute to personal valor in a specific New York City work setting. Anything else was coincidence. One man's betrayal was another's courage. Again: anything else was coincidence.

Betrayal was also a prominent motif of *Apocalypse Now.*

Its premise was that Brando's Kurtz had betrayed the Special Forces by going rogue, organizing a private army of Montagnards and waging his own war against the Vietcong from a Cambodian hideaway; he had also betrayed all rationality by, in the estimation of his erstwhile superiors, going insane, and who needed that kind of publicity for a war being waged for democracy? To counter this defection, Sheen's Willard was sent to assassinate him, no time for military niceties. On the way, however, Willard had betrayals of his own to deal with, leading to the self-defensive killing of men assigned to his mission. Not since the HUAC years had double-crossing been so patriotic.

As one character after another moaned his last, I waited for any question at all from Adam. But he was too engrossed to leave the realities of the jungle for banal clarifications, and I was pretty sure he had already come to answers to his questions in any case. Like everybody else tuned to the movie, he was primarily interested in what would happen when Willard and Kurtz finally came face to face. It was the romance in him, I thought. What I might have told him after the movie if I had been articulate enough was that some confrontations were inevitable, others not so much. Some were not even overt confrontations, but small seeds that dropped to earth as disappointments, sprouted jaundiced leaves under the soil, and one day blighted the garden. With Uncle Ralph, "that conscience thing" developed from age and generational outlook, was no excuse for fisticuffs on a waterfront shack and a subsequent Calvary trudge to redemption. One day I didn't want to buy his insurance policies, and he didn't want to sell me any; as simple as that. I was on my own. Get going; God bless on your travels. No romance, merely "that conscience thing."

Brando, on the other hand, lingered as pure romance in *On the Waterfront*. It didn't matter that he had portrayed a character loosely (again) based on a longshoreman who had ended up in the waters of New York harbor after defying the corrupt union. That wasn't Kazan's ending (for himself either), but as he had been at pains to say, coincidence was coincidence and could only go so far as one. In the meantime, not having to be fished out of harbor waters, Brando sat at the center of *Apocalypse Now* as a Johnny Friendly converted into Buddha. It was a little disorienting. He had trekked from Terry Malloy through Don Corleone to a gang leader who had Montagnards with him instead of Two-Ton Tony Galento and appeared unfazed by the journey. I might have abided that (eventually) if he had sat quietly despotic, making it clear that he knew why Willard was there and had been expecting somebody like him. But no, he insisted on some of that Conradian jabber from *Heart of Darkness*. With corpses he had reduced to that state only a few yards away, he wanted to talk about the human condition! The man's superiors were more right than they had known: Democracy, hypocrisy, and all the other ideologies aside, he *was* insane.

Kurtz was easy. In novels and screenplays, he was the purest of paper creations. But Brando gave life to more than that. You saw it in the glow in his eyes. He was a self-indulgent actor too skilled ever to be bad as in just bad, to be reciting "O Captain! My Captain!" for Mrs. Brown. As gargantuan as he had grown, he held on to the renegade instincts in Kurtz, delivering dialogue first as though in a town hall, then communing only with his soul before it flew away from his body. It was what the French call a *tour de force* and what others might relate to being a ham. You had to lean in like Willard to hear some of the mutterings, and that was part of the fugue, too, scored down to every note. Some torments elided words altogether, but he insisted on suggesting them anyway. It took me a minute to realize what was familiar about it—from *On the Waterfront* when Terry Malloy was confessing to Saint that he had played a role in her brother's murder and foghorns and whistles had drowned out what he had actually been saying. Some pains could not be confessed, ever, and if Brando's gross appearance and nostalgic abilities didn't compensate for that, there was very little lost when Sheen's Willard hacked him to death with a machete. No betrayal this time: just what everybody had expected. The horror of it all.

Leaving the movie house was like emerging into sunlight from the Cambodian jungle: Life had been going on elsewhere on earth familiarly, safely, sluggishly, and seemed smug about it.

"We never saw one like that before," Adam said, making me instantly gratified to be inside with him for thinking aloud.

"What did you think?"

He needed a second for that, and I hated a KFC wrapper for blowing along the sidewalk and maybe distracting him. "If Kurtz was so bad, killing all these people," he said finally, "how come he talked like he did, sounding even like you?"

I waited for the smile. It took forever. But at last, it came. That conscience thing kicking in.

DEATH IN VENICE

You don't have to join a religious cult or enlist in the Army to develop that communal *we* attitude toward life. I had it as far back as the fifth grade when I was a ringleader of the Black Arrows, a gang of a dozen classmates who assembled on a street corner a half-hour before the first bell to take on the enemy Musketeers. We didn't face off with guns, razors, or metal pipes; at most, we wielded wooden rulers for swords and used fists, with even the fists reduced to the pushing and pseudo-wrestling common to baseball diamond brawls. The point wasn't the weapons; it was the belonging. The occasional black eye honored the victim as much as the puncher.

Indeed, there was little more thrilling in fifth grade than blanketing a street block with friends grouping for the same adventurous purpose. It was even more so as a Black Arrow, a disreputable outlaw bunch, charging the respectable Musketeers with their Establishment associations. To go up the street in file with another Black Arrow was to discover some fellow renegade not evident behind a classroom desk or on a basketball court, an ally in trust and reliance. He might have been slow or brilliant in English and History, a terrific or a feeble dribbler, but none of that mattered when he chose to be a Black Arrow rather than a Musketeer and volunteered to be counted running up the block rather than down it. The suppositions in such alliances had never been spelled out, but there they were anyway.

But as gratifying as discovering an unexpected ally could be, the essence of being a Black Arrow was not in an individual adherent but in the congregation of purpose. Yes, numbers consolidated a sense of security, the same feeling of security at play in building and holing up in a snow fort after a blizzard and pulling up the ladder to a treehouse in the back yard. But there was more to it than that. What it ultimately celebrated was the fusion of the individual identified as an ally and the insignificance of that individual as such within our group ranks. Nobody was responsible for everything, but everybody assumed he was. Did that make for more pressure or less pressure? Being together was the priority; intellectual concerns could come later. Not even results weighed. To the undoubted disapproval of the cults rounding up converts and the armed forces toting up casualties, my notion of a *we* never even figured out if the Black Arrows or Musketeers emerged most often triumphant from our clashes.

I had few Black Arrow scenes in the decades to follow. Averse to shivs, uniforms, tattoos, red and green berets, tailgate hamburgers, and *omerta*, I navigated the time with a minimum of accomplices at a given moment. I was hardly a hermit., but I rarely thought of myself as part of some distinctively defining company. I did not need an ID badge and didn't ask my jacket handkerchief pocket to yield to one. Going to the ballgame *en masse* meant passing beers from the vendor down the row. Impersonal ritual commanded weddings and funerals. Going for drinks with colleagues after work said as much about the convenient location of the bar as about personal relations. Over years numerous enough to require a multiplication table, the most conspicuous exception occurred one year when my wife suggested we go to a restaurant for my birthday.

What Marta neglected to tell me was that she had also informed a few friends of our intention. About a block shy of our destination, I saw that the movie theater directly in front of the restaurant had just emptied out a show and was clogging the sidewalk with its patrons. Except they weren't people just released from the theater: They were friends and the friends of friends and friends of their friends who had come for what had started out as a quiet birthday dinner. How could chaos have that many notes—some tearfully embracing, others sardonic, yet others all but paralyzing? We didn't enter the restaurant; we occupied it. As befit the slowest to catch on, I worried that there would be room for everyone. As one used to dealing with dazes at surprise gatherings, the restaurant owner wished me so many Happy Birthdays I felt ten years older just standing inside his door.

The evening was loud and joyous—and ever so slightly off. The sheer number of people drawn up around an improvised table King Arthur would have envied reduced everyone to a cameo. The hors d'oeuvres were snatched, conversations were cribbed. The main course arrived but never really seemed to. Evasiveness wormed its way in, jokes lost their punchlines, but the alternative was to repeat an anecdote to the left already told on the right. In an odd diplomatic soiree fashion, we all became cocktail party guests for one another. Clearly, number alone was not all that it added up to be. A *we* had to be more than that. Over nostalgia for childhood games, it could even thrive on the very breaking of ranks. Being solitary wasn't the only alternative.

Several months later, Thomas Mann, Luchino Visconti, and Gustav Mahler showed why not.

I can't say I was enthusiastic about seeing Visconti's film version of Mann's novella *Death in Venice*. Especially after *The Leopard*, the director's most recent pictures—*The Stranger* and *The Damned*—had seemed like desperately barren exercises about barren people; if there was anybody Luchino Visconti felt at ease with, it wasn't Luchino Visconti. Add to that Mann's take on a finicky European society of the early 20th century in which pedophilia was given its head as artistic anguish but immediately apologized for with whores in bordellos, and Laurel and Hardy did not come to mind. Nevertheless, several of us gathered at the Cinema Giulio Cesare in Rome one evening with expectations of various kinds.

We were all armed. I had my wariness. Marta's addiction to Mann took the form of rereading *Joseph and His Brothers* or *Buddenbrooks* every other year. Journalist friend Piero couldn't have approved more since he was convinced that there was no worthy culture outside that seeded in Central Europe. Painter Daniel admitted fascination with Visconti's gilded elaborations, although he filled his canvasses with various shades of grim charcoal. Musician Cecily was ready to forgive Visconti for anything because of his operatic background. Economist Julian and trade union politician Nello were curious to see if a self-avowed communist director from an aristocratic family even remembered Karl Marx. From aesthetic tastes to political ideologies, the contradiction was in the air.

Visconti made one major change in the protagonist as played by Dirk Bogarde: Instead of the book's writer, Gustav von Aschenbach was turned into a composer, supposedly on the presumption that Mann had based the principal character on Mahler anyway. This pleased Cecily, annoyed Marta and Piero, and left Daniel to wander around the meticulously and brilliantly color-designed furnishings of the Lido hotel lobby in which much of the action was focused. For him, every piece was somebody's exotic obsession. For me, the lobby evoked a restaurant birthday dinner. It was spacious but still cluttered, mobbed but scarce. Widths didn't mesh with heights, heights with widths, or something. What was the opposite of lighting—darkening? Guests could sit recessed with an aperitif but looked to be in constant danger of bumping into others with whom they exchanged only trivial niceties. When a Polish aristocrat (Silvana Mangano) swept by with her militantly behaved children, her big dress alone jeopardized lamps, ashtrays, and slow-on-the-uptake guests. As hotel lobbies went, it was more of an overly appointed precipice than a social hub. You didn't really get to enjoy the hors d'oeuvres there, either.

Aschenbach might have become a composer in the Visconti makeover, but Bogarde's frail stares and a wayward jaw suggesting that he wasn't totally recovered from a numbing punch stressed the verbal even in his silence. He didn't have a tune in his head; he had sentences. And they weren't jovial sentences since he was in Venice in the first place in the hope that the Lido beach would help restore a weak heart. None of this fragility was helped by a suspiciously hasty checking out of hotel guests, the closing of shops without warning, and the manic reassurances of the hotel manager and others living on the tourist trade that there was nothing to worry about, that rumors of a cholera epidemic were nothing but empty talk. What every tremor of Aschenbach's body told you was that he knew empty talk better than anybody when he heard it.

Nello was the next to check out, and with Mangano as an alibi. He couldn't get over how beautiful she had remained so many decades after

Bitter Rice had made her Italy's international sex symbol or, not too long after that since she had vibrated Venice's dance floors in *Mambo*. A different Venice, as he whispered to Julian, from the one in which homoerotic impulses were beginning to stir n Aschenbach as the composer laid his eyes on Mangano's teenage son Tadzio. Julian grunted something along the lines of nothing being the same as it had been, not least himself, then someone in the row behind told them to go outside if they wanted to talk. Nello shut up about Mangano and returned to more immediate sex reveries.

Whatever Mann had intended through the character of Tadzio (Bjorn Andresen), an out-of-reach symbol of beauty and innocence, for instance, the harbinger of Aschenbach's death, another possibility, splintered with Visconti's offering of a spoiled teenager who had read something about turning on older men. He plainly turned on Aschenbach, for whom the sand and the sun at the beach were secondary to Tadzio's prancing around in his tight-fitting bathing costume. Ambiguity soured into malice, evoking *The Stranger* and *The Damned*. If Visconti liked any of the characters before the camera, he managed to disguise it better than their fears about the cholera epidemic. Even as they scrambled for distance, he epitomized it.

Marta slid down in her seat: Something was missing from the Mann novella, and it wasn't just words. Piero sensed her defection but kept his gaze on the screen expecting better Central European things. In another testament to perverse opposites, Daniel appeared happily distracted by the Lido's sea blues and cabana whites, neither color on his own palette and most commonly found together on the seascapes peddled in tourist souvenir shops. I wouldn't have minded a cigarette but didn't know what I had achieved to earn one. It wasn't simply the meanness that made it impossible to relax; it was the florid vehicle for trying to pass it off as aromatic depth. If Visconti's politics were anything like the treatment of his screen subjects, he would have been thrown out of the Communist Party as a fascist.

Aschenbach was coming to decision time. First, he persuaded himself that he wanted hard facts, that he wasn't just sagging as prey to his lust, so he pressured a squirrely clerk into conceding that the city was indeed harboring cholera. He was distraught to receive the confirmation, and not only because of the plague itself. Now he had to *act*, to choose between fleeing a disease especially dangerous to someone in his physical condition or staying put to get a few more glimpses and nurture a few more fantasies about Tadzio. Since the picture wasn't entitled *Merry Days in Venice*, he stayed.

Aschenbach would not benefit from a *deus ex machina*, but Visconti's film did. Doubling down on the decision to change the protagonist from a writer to a composer, it embarked on a lengthy sequence in which dialogue was all but banned while Aschenbach became a period caricature of the perfumed dandy, as much clown as a gentleman under a sinister barber's ministrations. And the circus-like makeup was only half of it: the sequence was scored by the tormenting *adagietto* of Mahler's *Fifth Symphony* as if to remind Mann who had allegedly inspired the story, to begin with. For ten minutes or more, the screen writhed to the magisterial soundtrack and lush colors of decay that succeeded in making the previously oppressive an inevitability meriting attention to a looming tragedy. Aschenbach and Tadzio were resistible, but not Mahler, and the imp cavorting on Venice's abandoned streets and bridges was a director rejoicing in how he had brought everything together despite even Mann's creative discretion. It was a wedding as a prelude to a funeral, with both celebrating humiliation.

What was left proceeded with a schematic ghoulishness. In his hideous makeup, Aschenbach watched Tadzio wrestle another teenager on the beach, continents removed from the visceral thrills of their physicality, staggered to his feet to follow Tadzio into the surf, then just keeled over and died of a heart attack. Tadzio was left pointing to some distant realm in the style of Greek gods or canned soup logos.

Given the big names attached to it and its presentation as a prestige picture, *Death in Venice was* useful for raising funds for slowing down the sinking of the Italian city. In a bar after the film, we could have used a few gondolas ourselves to stay afloat. Of course, the acting was good. (When wasn't it good if George Raft wasn't in it?) The photography would have made Venetian masters jealous. And the Mahler section? Cecily didn't have to argue her case. The rest of it had none of the conciseness of a novella. Marta and Piero were grateful for the encounter with Mann in the manner of obituary readers who opted to postpone annoyance over details out of a sense of decorum as much as a sense of futility. Daniel wore the perplexity of the spectator: an estrangement from excitements and disappointments and asking himself if he wanted to get any closer to them.

Then and there, I didn't appreciate the urgency of the talk between Nello and Julian about Visconti's politics. Shouldn't it have been obvious? After his earlier years with the nitty-gritty people of *The Earth Trembles* and *Rocco and His Brothers,* he had found it more comfortable decomposing the stuffy classes on the screen no matter how Compagno Luchino voted in Italian elections, right? For all its merits, hadn't *The Leopard* clearly marked that transition? It was the bourgeoisie that attended his operas, not the immigrant boxers of *Rocco and His Brothers.* What else was there to say?

Less and less about *Death in Venice.* It wasn't the only thing worth musing about. Piero was struck by how a modest Viale Giulio Cesare was about as good as it got in Rome for the would-be dictator so associated with the city; Handel and Shakespeare had shown more respect. That got Cecily into thinking how kaisers, shahs, and czars shared a root with a Caesarian birth sectioning. That didn't lead to consideration of Caesar salads and Kaiser rolls, but it could have. Lifted from Venice's narrow, sometimes precarious, streets, we had the whole world open for reconnoitering.

The *espresso* rounds became *prosecco* rounds. There was no rush to get to a car to get home. There was a murder only a couple of blocks away, a government scandal with the housing ministry, soccer, the discomforts of cabanas, Tuscan personalities versus Roman personalities, Czech music, the new popularity of the mandolin, Argentinian beef, a million-dollar robbery in San Diego, immigrants from the Philippines, the seediness of the Villa Borghese zoo, Trilussa, Vatican follies, another murder in Milan, high prices, even a return by Nello to Silvana Mangano's beauty. Bemused, heated, stubborn, peculiar, original—the observations flew out from the bar over Viale Giulio Cesare, first slamming into cars and taxis and buses but then just evaporating in the night's emptied avenue.

So many observations, so much control. The *we* had never been more *we*, almost to a smug degree.

I haven't been able to think of Mann or Visconti since that evening without seeing Daniel drawing on his sketch pad or hearing Julian go on about the filmmakers who didn't submit to Visconti's political trajectory. Most petrifying of all has been the playing of Mahler's *adagietto* on the radio. It no longer accompanies Aschenbach's fell into humiliation, but rather a lot of friends sitting around in a bar on Viale Giulio Cesare. They are all dead now, every single one of them, and none could blame Venice.

www.ingramcontent.com/pod-product-compliance
Lightning Source LLC
LaVergne TN
LVHW091009080826
845145LV00003B/1185

9781620068885